LONDON R[illegible]YS

Capital Transport

John Glover

Published by Capital Transport Publishing Ltd
www.capitaltransport.com

Printed by 1010 Printing International Ltd

CONTENTS

The area covered by this book is that of the Greater London Authority (GLA), extended judiciously to what might be termed the natural termini of inner-suburban services. Generally excluded are services which have minimal stops in that area, essentially those which might be termed InterCity or outer-suburban operations, open access operations (which apart from Heathrow Express all fall into the long distance category) and charter services.

The System

National Rail is the bedrock of the railway systems serving London; the first London terminus was that at London Bridge, opened in 1836. This was a small affair, soon to be dwarfed by the construction of the monumental station at Euston, which opened on 20 July 1837. Since then the number of termini, and the lines serving them, have blossomed, though it will be noted that only one line penetrates the central area to the extent of providing a connection between north and south. That is the route of the Thameslink service between Farringdon and Blackfriars. Another long standing and important connection is that of the West London Line (Willesden Junction and Clapham Junction), though as its name suggests this is far from central. An east-west penetrating line, Crossrail, will be fully opened in 2019.

The Department for Transport's stated aim is that the franchises for train operating companies (TOCs) should normally last between seven and ten years, with a pre-contracted continuation for a further three to five years subject to agreed criteria.

For each service, the operator and length of franchise or concession is given, an outline of the operation and services offered, the rolling stock used, the principal stations served, an indication of patronage, and likely future developments. Growth in the patronage of National Rail services, as with London Underground and other rail operations, is continuing at an unprecedented speed. The provision of adequate carrying capacity for future needs with a growing population is thus a major preoccupation of planners and operators alike.

Freight operations are mentioned to the extent that they have a substantial impact on the operation of passenger services.

No 455.710, which looks as if it could do with a visit to a carriage washer, passes Putney with an up Waterloo roundabout service on 25 May 2013. The second vehicle comes from a Class 508 unit and the different profile is readily apparent. On the up side 455.903 is receding into the distance. *Chris Wilson*

Presentation

Railways are considered in geographical order, starting with the Tilbury line on the north side of the River Thames and then anti-clockwise until reaching the south side and services to Dartford, followed by London Overground. The operations of each Train Operating Company are discussed separately.

The timetables relating to present National Rail services are those in force from May 2014 to December 2014, unless stated otherwise. This minimises the effects of the huge London Bridge rebuilding, which from the beginning of 2015 has resulted in frequent service changes and will do so for some time to come.

The basic services described are those operating at off-peak. These are defined as those operating on Mondays to Fridays in the hour starting at 12:00. That service pattern is often repeated on Saturdays, and on a less frequent basis on Sundays. Space does not permit an account of the varying service levels during the Monday to Friday peaks, though these are sometimes mentioned, and all services are assessed in the 'from London' direction only. That in the reverse direction may usually be taken as a mirror image.

Service frequencies are referred to as trains per hour (tph). Note that this expression does not mean that trains run at equal intervals, such as 00, 15, 30, 45 mins past each hour (4 tph), though they may often do so. Trains at 00, 05, 30, 35 will still be 4 tph; such a result is less than desirable, but it may sometimes be necessary due to other timetabling constraints.

Maps are included where they may be useful, but the London-wide rail system is so complex that reproduction of the London Connections map at this page size would be of very little value. This map is freely available at London railway stations and often outside the capital also.

Station usage

Overall usage statistics for National Rail stations are published by the Office of Rail & Road and some are mentioned in the text. That usage is the combined total of all station entries and station exits. All passengers are included, not merely those making journeys within the area covered by this book.

As might be expected, the main London terminals head the list of busy stations, though not exclusively so. Notably, it is the southern suburbs in the arc from the south west round to east London that feature most strongly, rather than those in the sector from the west to the north. In the latter, London Underground operations are much more strongly represented.

Perhaps surprising is the strength of the London Overground showing, given the somewhat chequered history of the services concerned. However, a station shown as being managed by one operator does not in itself preclude others from using it. Thus Clapham Junction is managed by South West Trains, but much use of it is made by Southern and also London Overground.

Journey lengths on National Rail are likely to be longer than those on the Underground of around five miles. The average fares paid are also that much higher. Thus commuting the 50 miles from either Brighton or Bedford to London using Thameslink is eminently possible, but it is not a cheap option!

London Overground is becoming a major element of London's railways and so far all of its electric stock bought new has been of similar design. Whitechapel station was formerly part of London Underground's East London line and as part of today's Overground passes beneath the Underground's District line. *Kim Rennie*

National Express hold the present Essex Thameside franchise for a 15-year term, 2014 to 2029. This is the route of the former London, Tilbury & Southend Railway, but the present company trades as c2c.

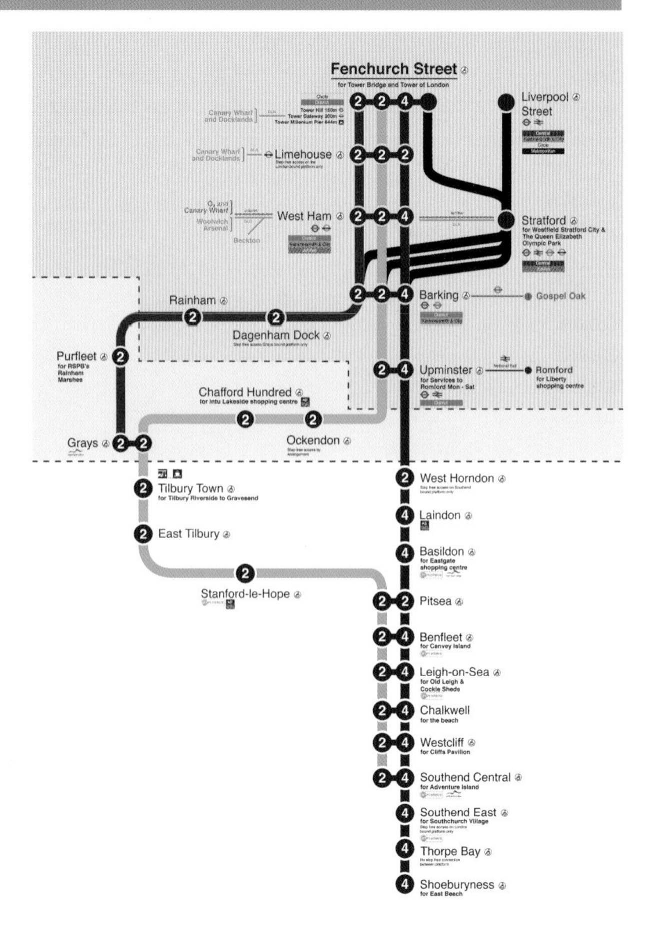

Route

This is an outer-suburban service from Fenchurch Street to the Southend area. The main route is via Basildon and within the GLA calls are made at Limehouse, West Ham, Barking and Upminster.

A secondary route runs from Barking via Grays and Tilbury, rejoining the main line at Pitsea. This has Greater London stations at Dagenham Dock and Rainham. Yet a third line diverges at Upminster running via Ockendon and Chafford Hundred to Grays, but the branch stations are outside the GLA.

This is basically a double track railway, with junctions at grade. The sole exception is that of the flyovers at Barking, which keep freight traffic separated from the main line.

London Underground services operate on the north side of the formation from Campbell Road, just short of Bromley-by-Bow, to Upminster. These are completely separate tracks, other than a connection for engineering purposes at Barking.

The busiest stations are Fenchurch Street (18 million passengers joining and alighting in 2014), Barking (8m) and Upminster (5m).

Timetable

The standard off peak timetable offers 8 tph departing from London. These run via Basildon (4 tph), Ockendon (2 tph) or Rainham (2 tph). These are basically all stations services, with very few exceptions. Stops may be omitted on (say) alternate services.

Saturday services are similar, but on Sundays are reduced to 4 tph from Fenchurch Street. The service to Grays via Rainham becomes an hourly shuttle from Barking.

This is a heavily peaked service. On Monday to Friday evenings between 17:00 and 17:59, 20 trains leave Fenchurch Street. Some are limited stop, notably two Shoeburyness trains which run non-stop to Benfleet. All the main line intermediate stations in Greater London see some stations omitted on occasion. A small number of trains are diverted west of Barking to run to Stratford and Liverpool Street.

Trains

All trains are formed from a fleet of 46 Class 357/0 4-car units of Derby-built AdTranz/Bombardier Electrostars dating from 1999, and the follow-on order of 28 very similar Class 357/2s. They are Standard Class only.

These are 20m long air-conditioned open vehicles, with 3+2 seating either side of a central gangway. Layout is a mixture of facing and uni-directional. Sliding plug doors are provided, two sets for each side of each car body. End corridor connections to an adjacent unit are provided. Each unit has 278 seats plus 4 tip-up, 2 wheelchair spaces and 1 disabled toilet.

Peak formations may be formed of up to 12-cars (3x4-car units). While platforms on the main line via Basildon can accommodate 12-car trains, most of those elsewhere are restricted to 8-cars (2x4-car units).

The 357/0s are leased from Porterbrook ROSCO, the 357/2s from Angel Trains. Maintenance is carried out at East Ham EMU depot to which all trains are allocated; there are also extensive carriage sidings, with a carriage washer, at Shoeburyness.

Control

All services on what is known collectively as 'the Tilbury' are controlled from the Integrated Electronic Control Centre (IECC) at Upminster.

Franchise commitments

Operator commitments under the current franchise include the provision of 17 new 4-car trains and a significant upgrade to the existing fleet, with 20% more trains from December 2015. New smartcards, flexible season tickets, carnets, etc, plus investment in stations will make c2c services fully accessible, and a quarter of weekend services will serve Stratford and Liverpool Street.

All c2c trains, providing services out of Fenchurch Street station, are now in the white livery of the current franchise holder National Express. A 357/0 is seen at Shadwell. *Capital Transport*

GREATER ANGLIA

The Greater Anglia services franchise run by Abellio was extended to terminate in October 2016, with additional service quality conditions. A new Greater Anglia long-term franchise is in the course of letting.

Routes

This franchise was much altered from 31 May 2015, with the loss of nearly all the inner suburban operations to either London Overground or Crossrail. Remaining is the route that runs from London Liverpool Street via Tottenham Hale and the Lea Valley to Broxbourne, thence to Hertford East.

Outer suburban services run on the Great Eastern main line from London Liverpool Street line to Shenfield and beyond (Southend Victoria, Colchester etc), plus services to Stansted Airport or Cambridge. The Greater London boundaries fall beyond the stations at Enfield Lock or Harold Wood.

Interchanges with London Underground are confined to Liverpool Street, Stratford and Tottenham Hale, and also with both London Overground and the Docklands Light Railway (two separate routes) at Stratford.

Liverpool Street handles 63 million passengers a year and Tottenham Hale 5 million.

Great Eastern main line

The only Monday to Friday off-peak services to call at both Stratford and Romford continue to Colchester Town (1 tph) or to Southend Victoria (1 tph). Outer-suburban trains are primarily the 4-car Class 321 units (84 sets) and the 4-car Class 360 Siemens Desiro units (21 sets). All are 20m vehicles, have two classes of travel, and are maintained at Ilford.

Control

The line is controlled by Liverpool Street IECC which fringes with Colchester beyond Marks Tey station. The main line is 4-tracked as far as Shenfield, thence double track to Southend Victoria and towards Colchester.

Freight

There is substantial container traffic to and from the ports at Harwich and Felixstowe, much of which is routed via Stratford and the North London Line.

On 12 May 2015, Abellio Greater Anglia's no 317.506 in the red door livery is seen at Rectory Road. *Capital Transport*

Lea Valley

The off peak timetable Mondays to Fridays offers a 2 tph service to Hertford East via the Lea Valley, with calls at Hackney Downs, Tottenham Hale, Ponders End and then all stations. Further services run at 2 tph from Stratford to Bishops Stortford, skip-stopping on the Lea Valley, though Angel Road has no off-peak service. Stansted Airport fast services run at 4 tph and Cambridge services at 2 tph, but none of these call at other than Tottenham Hale in Greater London.

During the Monday to Friday evening peak from 17:00 to 17:59, there are 2 fast services to Hertford East, calling at Hackney Downs, Seven Sisters, Edmonton Green, Cheshunt and then all stations.

On the Lea Valley, Stansted Airport services remain the same, but Cambridge services are up to 4 tph. Liverpool Street to Broxbourne runs at 2 tph, calling at principal stations. Of the 2 services from Stratford to Bishops Stortford, one is diverted to Hertford East. On Saturdays there are 2 tph from Liverpool Street to Hertford East via Tottenham Hale, plus the 2 tph Stratford to Bishops Stortford service but with fewer stops. The local services on Sundays are decidedly thin and one of the two Cambridge services starts from Stratford to provide an hourly service stopping at Tottenham Hale, Ponders End and then all stations. And that is it.

Trains

Trains used are the Class 317s, constructed originally by BR Engineering from 1981, mostly at York. The 4-car sets of 20m vehicles have been variously rebuilt. All have some 1st class accommodation. They are leased from Angel Trains and are based at Ilford. These are outer-suburban units with end gangway connections; two sets of double sliding doors per vehicle side.

The Class 379s are 20m 4-car Electrostar vehicles built by Bombardier, Derby, in 2010. These too have mixed 1st and Standard Class accommodation and are used on the longer distance services including Stansted Expresses. There are 30 sets, maintained at Ilford, and leased from the Macquarie Group.

Control

All lines are controlled by Liverpool Street IECC, which interfaces with Cambridge at Elsenham, 35 miles from London.

No 317.666 of Abellio Greater Anglia in the unattractive grey and white livery applied to 317/7 units stands with its doors open at Liverpool Street in May 2015. Most trains are now receiving white livery with red doors. *Capital Transport*

The Thameslink, Southern & Great Northern franchise began on 14 September 2014. Since then it has absorbed some Southeastern services, with all Southern services following on 26 July 2015 when that franchise expired.

The TS&GN franchise was won by GoVia, for a seven year term until September 2021. This is a management contract style franchise, due to the extensive and complex works under way at (notably) London Bridge but also elsewhere.

The physical link between St Pancras International low level station via Canal Tunnel to the Great Northern, south of the Copenhagen Tunnels, has yet to be commissioned. This will enable Thameslink trains from south London to run through to destinations served by the Great Northern, as opposed to the Midland only as at present.

Great Northern Moorgate services

The Great Northern inner-suburban services form part of the franchise run by Thameslink & Great Northern.

Moorgate on the former Great Northern & City Underground line was established as the London terminus of Great Northern suburban services, with the completion of the British Rail suburban electrification scheme in 1976. It has 9 million passengers a year. Of the other Great Northern stations, King's Cross has 30 million passengers a year, Highbury & Islington 16m (includes Overground) and Finsbury Park 6m.

Route

Trains run from the wholly underground terminus, calling at Old Street, Essex Road, Highbury & Islington and Drayton Park. Here the line emerges from tunnel and this is where the pantograph is raised and 25kV AC electrification takes the place of third-rail 750v DC. Burrowing junctions take the trains to the main line at Finsbury Park, which is aligned down slow, down fast, up fast, up slow. Trains may call at Harringay, Hornsey and Alexandra Palace, after which those to Hertford North leave by a flyover.

Stations thence are Bowes Park, Palmers Green, Winchmore Hill, Grange Park, Enfield Chase, Gordon Hill and Crews Hill, after which the line is in Hertfordshire. On the main line, the part in Greater London calls at New Southgate, Oakleigh Park, New Barnet and Hadley Wood, followed by Potters Bar and stations to Welwyn Garden City.

Passengers for the West End rather than the City are able to transfer to the Victoria line Underground by cross-platform interchange at Highbury & Islington, and nowadays a wide range of other destinations that can be reached by London Overground from the surface level platforms. Transfer to the Piccadilly is available at Finsbury Park.

Timetable

Today, the Moorgate services run Mondays to Fridays only, but before 06:30 and after 22:00 and all day Saturdays and Sundays trains are diverted to run from the three suburban platforms (9-11) of King's Cross main line station.

The basic Monday to Friday off-peak service runs alternately to Welwyn Garden City and to Hertford North. Once an hour, a Hertford North train is extended to Stevenage. All trains call at all stations. In the peaks the service consists of 12 tph from Moorgate, with 4 tph all stations to Welwyn Garden City and 8 tph to the branch. These terminate at Gordon Hill, Hertford North or Stevenage, with some skip stopping. Harringay and Hornsey are those omitted most often, but they are served also by the Welwyn Garden City services.

At weekends, a 2 tph service runs from King's Cross, alternately to Welwyn Garden City and Hertford North, with one of the latter extended to Stevenage.

Trains

Operation remains solely in the hands of the original dual-voltage Class 313/0 fleet of 3-car units, dating from 1976. They are often run as 6-car trains, the maximum length that can be accommodated at the underground stations.

The fleet consisted originally of 64 units, but 44 are sufficient to maintain the present operation. A further unit is used by Network Rail for ERTMS testing on the Hertford Loop, but the remainder now operate Southern Coastway services.

These are 20m-long open vehicles, now with high backed seats but retaining the 3+2 seating layout. They are Standard Class only. Sliding doors are provided, two sets for each side of each car body. The units have end doors but are gangwayed within the unit only. Each of the forty-one 313/0s has 271 seats; there are no toilets. There are also three very similar Class 313/1s.

The 313/0s are leased from Eversholt ROSCO. Maintenance is carried out at Hornsey EMU depot, to which all trains are allocated. There are also sidings at Welwyn Garden City.

Control

The whole of the suburban area is under the control of King's Cross Power Signal Box until it interfaces with Peterborough (north of Biggleswade) or Cambridge (beyond Royston).

Great Northern King's Cross services

Most of the services starting from King's Cross are in the outer-suburban category with 1st/Standard class. Many of these make calls at Finsbury Park and then with very few exceptions not again before Potters Bar. From here, most will continue to either Cambridge (58 miles) or Peterborough (76 miles), calling at all principal stations.

A Monday to Friday peak only service is the 2 tph from King's Cross to Welwyn Garden City. These trains call at Finsbury Park, New Southgate, Oakleigh Park, New Barnet, Potters Bar and Hatfield and are Standard Class only.

No 319.001 sports the new Govia Thameslink Railway livery at Kentish Town. This is the former Moorgate line, though today it exists only as far as Farringdon before going south. *Kim Rennie*

The key component of the TS&GN franchise is the reconstructed central section between Farringdon and Blackfriars. At one time a freight link, it fell into disuse and the track was lifted. The line was rebuilt and reopened initially in 1988 to carry what became Thameslink passenger services. City Thameslink station was built new in 1990, replacing the Holborn Viaduct terminus, which was closed.

Latterly, Thameslink services have run from Bedford, via the Midland Main Line, to the long standing connection to the Metropolitan Widened Lines. This took them to Farringdon and thence to Blackfriars. Here services diverged, to serve London Bridge, thence to Gatwick Airport and Brighton, or to Herne Hill, Tulse Hill and the Wimbledon/Sutton loop. This led to the abandonment of the main St Pancras station as a terminus for local services.

Route

The Midland is a 4-track main line arranged down fast, up fast, down slow, up slow. The line from Farringdon, which is mostly in tunnel, joins the slow lines at Kentish Town. Electrification of all these lines is at 25kV AC and extends from Farringdon to Bedford (50 miles).

Timetable

The basic Monday to Friday off-peak service in the summer timetable consists of 10 tph leaving Farringdon towards Bedford. All call at St Pancras Thameslink. All-stations trains to St Albans City run at 4 tph, 2 tph of which are extended to Luton. These call at West Hampstead Thameslink, Cricklewood, Hendon, Mill Hill Broadway (the last station in London) then Elstree & Borehamwood and stations to St Albans City/Luton. One of the latter continues to Bedford. There is a further 4 tph service to St Albans City and all stations to Bedford, 2 tph of which call also at West Hampstead Thameslink. A further 2 tph reverse at Kentish Town.

In the evening peak, the number of services increases to 13 tph, with all stations to St Albans City still at 4 tph but only 1 tph extended to Luton. Of the remaining 7 tph, two call at West Hampstead Midland and Mill Hill Broadway and all stations to St Albans City (or Bedford); all the rest are non-stop to St Albans City.

On Saturdays the off peak service is repeated but at 8 tph in total, being minus the Kentish Town terminators. Sundays see a further reduction to 5 tph, with 1 tph all stations to St Albans City. The remaining 4 tph call at West Hampstead Thameslink, St Albans City and all stations to Bedford.

Trains

Thameslink trains are primarily the BR York built 4-car Class 319s, totalling 86 units but with various revampings since their construction in 1987. With some, the 1st class seating has been removed. These trains are slowly making their way to new electrification schemes in the north of England.

They are supplemented by the 23 4-car Class 377/5 Electrostars from Bombardier, Derby, built in 2008 and sub-leased by Southern until the new Class 700 trains for Thameslink are delivered. All are dual voltage 25kV AC/750v DC units leased from the Porterbrook ROSCO. Cauldwell EMU depot is at Bedford, separated from most of the stabling sidings by the River Great Ouse.

Control

At present, control throughout is by West Hampstead Power Signal Box.

The Class 377s might be termed temporary visitors to Thameslink, but 377.512 sports full First Group livery at Kentish Town in April 2015. *Kim Rennie*

Kentish Town
377 512

Perhaps tellingly, the franchise operated by the GoVia company London Midland is referred to by the Department for Transport as that for the West Midlands. This is where the majority of its operations are, to which is added the extension to London Euston. This franchise, begun in 2007, runs to June 2017.

Route

London Midland operate the secondary (but not the local) services from London Euston, essentially those on the slow lines of what is basically a 4-track railway. For services on the so called DC lines, see the London Overground section.

The company's only regular intermediate calling point in Greater London is at Harrow & Wealdstone. Further calls are in Hertfordshire at Bushey and Watford Junction, and stations thence to Tring and beyond.

The whole is electrified at 25kV AC.

Timetable

The London area off-peak operation on Mondays to Fridays consists of 2 tph semi-fast services from Euston to Tring, calling at all stations from Harrow & Wealdstone.

Southern operate a 1tph service from South Croydon to Milton Keynes Central. This runs via the West London Line, calling on the common section at Wembley Central, Harrow & Wealdstone, Watford Junction, and stations north, but not Bushey.

The Southern service stays the same during the afternoon peak on Mondays to Fridays, though the London Midland service from Euston increases to 4 tph with a variety of terminating points.

At weekends the off-peak pattern is broadly maintained, though on Sundays the Southern service operates between Clapham Junction and Watford Junction only; the Wembley Central stop is omitted.

Trains

London Midland have a fleet of 77 Siemens Desiro Class 350 4-car emus with which these services are provided. These are leased from Angel/Porterbrook. There are also a few Class 321/4 4-car emus leased from Eversholt. All are based and maintained at Northampton, with off-peak stabling at Camden.

Control

This network is controlled by Wembley Main Line Signalling Control Centre.

London Midland's no 350.232 is seen arriving at Harrow & Wealdstone with an up service to London Euston on 30 May 2015. *Chris Wilson*

Chiltern services are operated by Arriva Trains DB under a franchise dating back to 3 March 2002. This runs until December 2021, with a possible further five year extension to run until 2026 by mutual agreement.

Routes

The line from London Marylebone diverges at (the flat) Neasden Junction, with one route continuing to Aylesbury and the other towards High Wycombe and Birmingham. Harrow-on-the-Hill (9 miles) is the only intermediate station within Greater London on the route to Aylesbury, though that to High Wycombe has Wembley Stadium (6 miles), Sudbury & Harrow Road, Sudbury Hill Harrow, Northolt Park, South Ruislip and West Ruislip (13 miles). This is in effect a double track railway.

London Marylebone handles around 15 million passengers a year.

Timetable

The Monday to Friday off peak Aylesbury trains run at 2 tph. Beyond Harrow-on-the-Hill they call at Rickmansworth, Chorleywood, Chalfont & Latimer and Amersham (23 miles). The tracks here are owned by London Underground's Metropolitan line, and the two operators provide a form of joint service. Chiltern trains continue thence all stations to Aylesbury.

However, the Metropolitan makes 13 stops between Baker Street and Amersham, Chiltern Railways make 4 stops on the journey from London Marylebone. Time by Metropolitan is 57 mins, that by Chiltern 35 mins. So clear win for Chiltern? Perhaps, but the Metropolitan offers rather better interchange with the rest of the Underground system, and this will be important for many.

In Monday to Friday peaks, Chiltern departures are doubled to 4 tph, with 2 tph running non-stop to Great Missenden.

The off peak service is the same on Saturdays, but reduced to 1 tph on Sundays.

On the High Wycombe route, the off peak service runs at 2 tph, alternately to High Wycombe and to Gerrards Cross. In Greater London, one stops at Wembley Stadium and South Ruislip, the other at Sudbury Hill Harrow, Northolt Park and West Ruislip.

The peak service shows little change, though Sudbury & Harrow Road does have 1 tph stopping there.

On Saturdays and Sundays, Wembley Stadium sees 2 tph, while Northolt Park and the following stations have a 1 tph service.

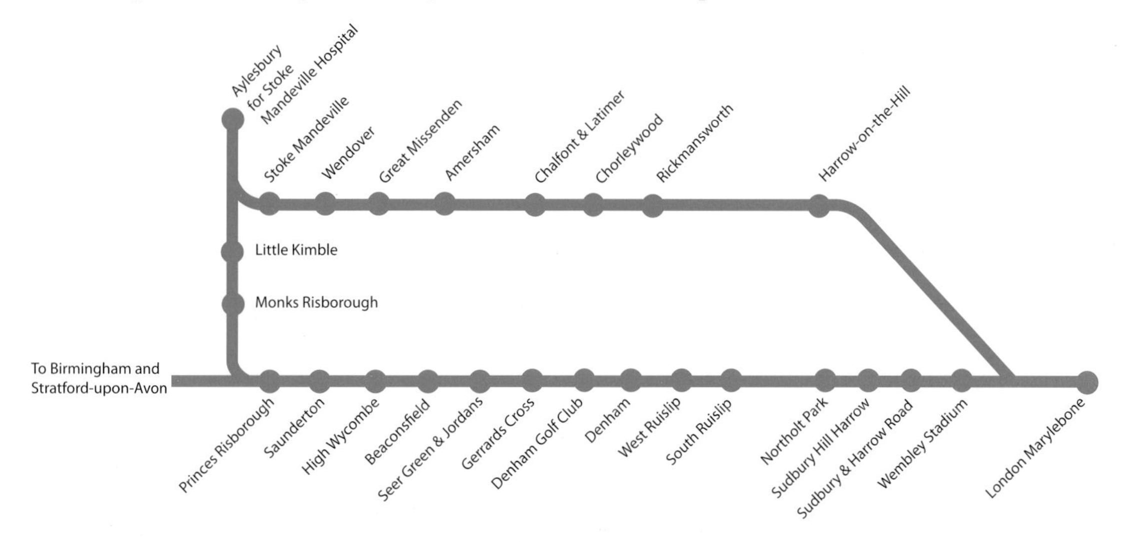

Trains

Chiltern Railways have a fleet of 39 Class 165/0 Networker Turbos (some 3-car, some 2-car); these were built in 1990. Additionally, there are 19 Class 168 Clubman (some 4-car, some 3-car, 3 different builds 1997-2003). There are also 4 2-car sets of Class 172/1 Turbostars, built in 2010. All have bodyshells of around 23m in length.

The three main ROSCOs own various parts of the fleet, all of which is based at Aylesbury.

Chiltern Railways do not have the traditional distinction between 1st and Standard class in the accommodation offered.

Part of the fleet is fitted with tripcocks to enable it to operate over London Underground owned lines between Harrow-on-the-Hill and Amersham. None of the Chiltern line itself is electrified.

Control

All lines from Marylebone are controlled by Network Rail's Marylebone Area Signalling Centre, other than the section under London Underground's Baker Street Signalling & Control Centre. Trains to Aylesbury thus 'disappear' from Network Rail signallers' view on reaching Harrow, to 'reappear' beyond Amersham.

After dark at Harrow-on-the-Hill on 31 October 2014 stands Chiltern Railways no 165.014. *Jason Cross*

A down service from London Marylebone with Chiltern Railways' 168.004 passing Neasden on 2 April 2015. On reaching Harrow-on-the-Hill the former Great Central Railway tracks merge with those of the Underground. In the background can be seen Neasden LU station, with a Jubilee line train. The new livery was introduced by Chiltern Railways in 2013. *Chris Wilson*

The Great Western franchise is held by First Great Western with a directly awarded mini-franchise which started in October 2013. This has already been extended until April 2019 and a further extension until July 2020 is possible. This takes account of many large scale capital works presently under way, including electrification, resignalling, Crossrail and Reading rebuilding.

At the same time, Heathrow Express is an open access operator, owned by the airport authority. There is also a joint venture between the two companies of the Heathrow Connect local service from Paddington.

Route

The Great Western main line extends west from London Paddington, reaching the Greater London boundary beyond West Drayton (13 miles). It then continues via Slough and Maidenhead to Reading (36 miles). This is a 4-track railway, arranged down fast, up fast, down relief, up relief; (nothing is ever 'slow' on the Great Western).

In the London area there is the branch from West Ealing to Greenford (9 miles). Beyond Hayes & Harlington the Heathrow Airport owned branch diverges to Terminals 1,2,3 (15 miles) followed by Terminal 4 or separately to Terminal 5. This branch, and the associated line from Paddington, is the only current usage of electric traction (25kV AC) on the Great Western.

Other than Paddington, Ealing Broadway is the busiest Great Western station in Greater London, with 5 million passengers a year.

Timetable

Electric services to Heathrow operate as follows on Mondays to Saturdays:

- Heathrow Express 4 tph from Paddington to Heathrow Terminals 1-2 and Heathrow Terminal 5. In addition, a shuttle service meets all trains and operates between Heathrow Terminals 1-2 and Heathrow Terminal 4 only.
- Heathrow Connect 2 tph from Paddington to Ealing Broadway and all stations to Heathrow Terminals 1-2 (only).

A slightly abbreviated service operates on Sundays.

The following are operated using First Great Western diesel units from Paddington during the Monday to Friday off-peak. There are 2 tph to Ealing Broadway, Hayes & Harlington, West Drayton and most stations to Reading and Oxford, and a further 2 tph to Ealing Broadway, Southall, Hayes & Harlington, West Drayton, Slough and all stations to Reading.

There is also a 2 tph service calling at all stations to Greenford, but this is to become a shuttle operation from the new bay platform at West Drayton in late 2015.

Monday to Friday peak variations amount to very little, with no extra trains. There is some shuffling of stopping patterns, but little else.

The Saturday service is similar to the Monday-Friday off peak.

Trains

First Great Western have 39 Class 165/1 Network Turbos, some 3-car sets and some 2-car. These 23m vehicles were built in 1992, as were 21 generally similar but rather classier Class 166 Network Express Turbos. These are 3-car units which include 1st class seating. All are leased from Angel Trains and are maintained at Reading.

First Great Western 2-car unit 165.123 passes Royal Oak on the Greenford to Paddington service. *Kim Rennie*

On 9 April 2014 First Great Western 3-car set 166.204 is seen on a service between Reading and Gatwick Airport approaching Guildford. *Chris Wilson*

HEATHROW EXPRESS

Heathrow Express own the Class 332 units built for their services by CAF from 1997. There are 9x5-car sets, and 5x4-car sets, using 23m vehicles These are based and maintained at Old Oak Common, as are the five 4-car Class 360/2 Siemens Desiro trains for the Heathrow Connect service. These are Standard class only.

Right: A Heathrow Express leaves Paddington. This is one of the trains in an all-over advert livery. *Capital Transport*

Below: The Vodafone brand is in bolder lettering than the Heathrow Express logo in this view. Note the level platform to train access on this service. *Capital Transport*

Inside the Heathrow Express trains, Standard Class areas coaches have 2+2 seating and first class have 1+1 seating. *Capital Transport*

Southall sees an up Heathrow Connect service in its distinctive livery, arriving at Southall. This is unit 360.202. Behind the train can be seen Southall's water tower, now converted into flats. In use from 1895 to 1968, it was the source of water for steam locomotives and was known locally as Southall Castle. Heathrow Connect is a joint venture between First Great Western and Heathrow Express, and travel on it is considerably cheaper than the non-stop services. *Chris Wilson*

South West Trains (SWT) is a Stagecoach company, whose franchise now runs until February 2017. The company has held this franchise since the initial privatisations.

Route

This is still essentially the operation of the London & South Western Railway from London Waterloo, as further improved by its Southern Railway successors. There are essentially two groups of routes: those associated with the main line towards Woking, and the Windsor lines. The most distant stations within Greater London are Hampton, Surbiton, Chessington South and Worcester Park, plus Feltham on the Windsor lines. This is a 3rd rail 750v DC railway, though services operated by diesel units from Exeter and Salisbury do continue through to Waterloo.

London Waterloo is the busiest station in Britain, with 98.4million passengers annually. Other busy SWT stations in Greater London are Clapham Junction with 25m, Vauxhall and Wimbledon both with 19m, Putney, Richmond and Surbiton with 10m and followed by Kingston, Earlsfield and Twickenham with 6m.

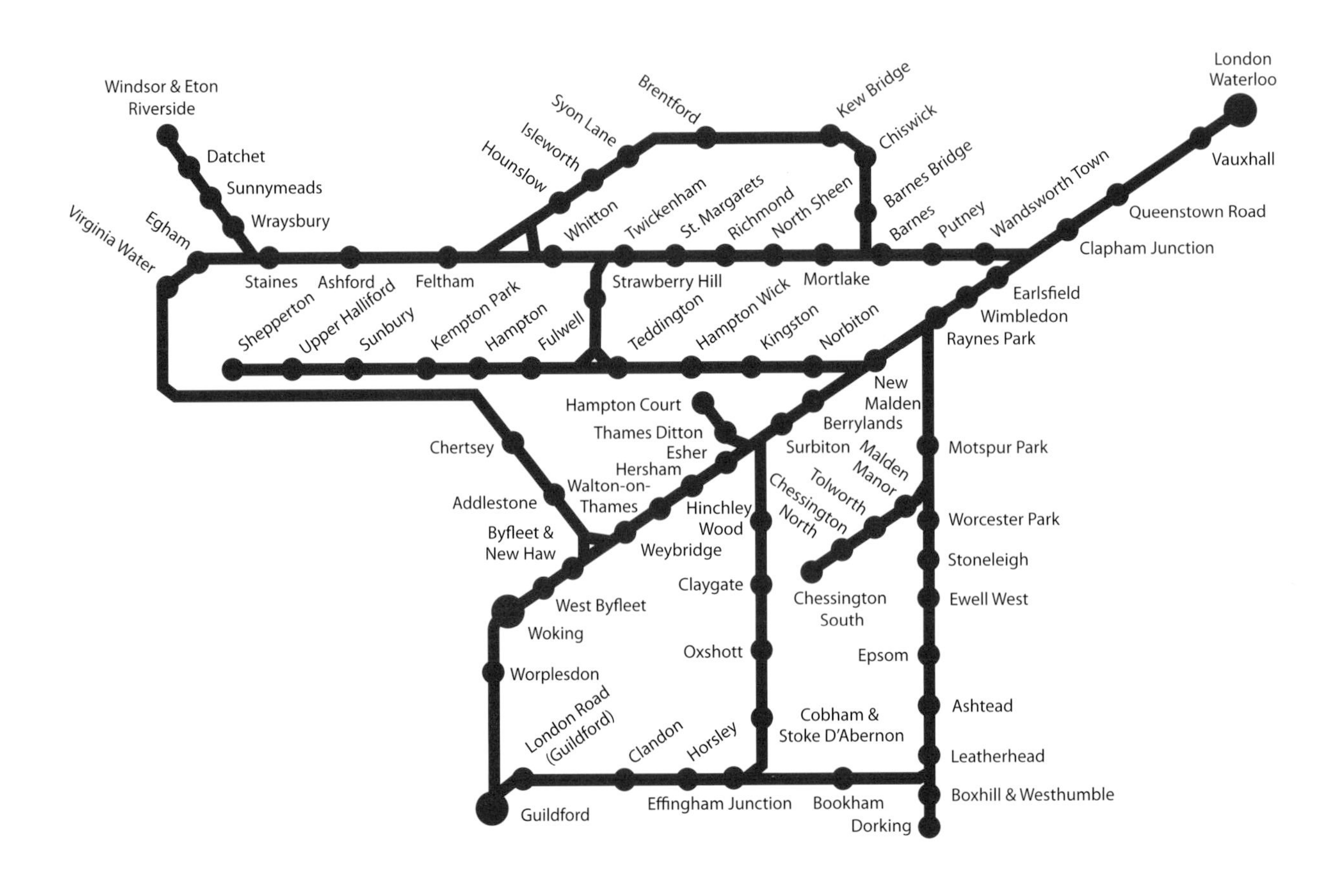

Timetable

On the Windsor lines, 12 tph leave London Waterloo in the midday off peak, Monday to Friday. These are six 2 tph pairs, consisting of 2 tph semi-fasts to Reading calling at Clapham Junction, Richmond, Twickenham, Feltham, Staines and all stations except Longcross. There are also 2 tph to Windsor & Eton Riverside, which add in a Putney stop to the above and run all stations from Twickenham. A third 2 tph service is that to Weybridge. This calls at all stations via Hounslow.

More locally, there are 2 tph all stations trains via Richmond to Kingston and back to Waterloo via Wimbledon. There are also 4 tph from Waterloo to Whitton; these run out alternately via Richmond and via Hounslow, then back to Waterloo by the 'other' route. These services are what have been called the roundabout routes.

In the evening peak hour on Monday to Friday there are 16 departures, consisting broadly of the above with some modest skip stopping, plus an extra train to Reading and another to Aldershot (via Ascot). There is an additional train to Waterloo via Kingston, and a second via Strawberry Hill to Shepperton. On Saturdays the off-peak Monday to Friday service is operated. On Sundays a simplified pattern is offered and what becomes the hourly service via Hounslow continues via Staines to Addlestone and Woking; the section to Weybridge is omitted. There are no Hounslow loop services, as such.

SWT refurbished class 458/0 units 8017/24 pass under the Wimbledon branch of the District line at Putney on a service from Reading to London Waterloo on 30 April 2015, its Greater London stopping points being Feltham, Twickenham, Richmond and Clapham Junction. *Chris Wilson*

The off-peak Monday to Friday stopping services on the main line run at 16 tph, as follows. These are essentially all stations services, though the last two groups omit Raynes Park, New Malden and Berrylands.

- 2 tph to Chessington South
- 4 tph to Epsom, then alternately Dorking and Guildford
- 2 tph to Hampton Court
- 2 tph to Kingston and back via Richmond to Waterloo
- 2 tph to Shepperton
- 2 tph to Guildford via Cobham
- 2 tph to Woking

Between 17:00 and 17:59, there is some modest service strengthening.

On Saturdays the off peak timetable applies. On Sundays, most service frequencies are halved, with only Chessington South, Hampton Court and Woking services (extended to Guildford) retaining their weekday frequencies. This reduces the total trains leaving Waterloo to 10 tph.

Trains

South West Trains have a large fleet of the 4-car Class 455 units (43 Class 455/7, 37 Class 455/8 and 20 Class 455/9) built at York 1982-1985. These 20m vehicles with two double doors per vehicle side are the stalwarts of the inner suburban services. To these can be added the similar 24 Class 456 2-car units dating from 1990 and recently acquired from Southern. These will assist in the eventual aim of all inner-suburban trains being able to operate with 10-cars.

London Waterloo on 10 March 2014 sees 458.531 of South West Trains in the Windsor line platforms. This unit has been made up to five cars with the addition of a vehicle from the now disbanded Class 460 Gatwick Express fleet. *Kim Rennie*

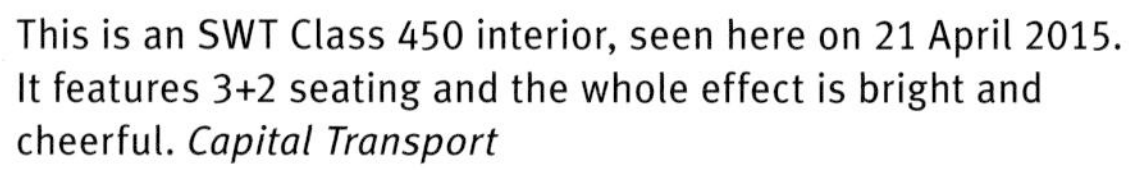

This is an SWT Class 450 interior, seen here on 21 April 2015. It features 3+2 seating and the whole effect is bright and cheerful. *Capital Transport*

They do so in conjunction with the 30 Class 458 Alstom Juniper 4-car trains, presently in the process of being reconfigured as 36 Class 458/5 5-car units by being combined with the former Gatwick Express Class 460s.

Class 450s Siemens Desiro units of 4-cars, dating from 2002, operate the Reading services.

A new build of 30 5-car Class 707 Desiro City trains from Siemens will be delivered from 2017.

Wimbledon Train Care Depot is the main London area maintenance and stabling centre, supplemented in Greater London by facilities at Clapham Yard.

Control

Much of the London area, including Waterloo, is controlled by Wimbledon Area Signalling Centre (ASC). This interfaces on the Windsor lines with Feltham ASC at Chiswick/North Sheen and on the Kingston loop at Norbiton. Wimbledon interfaces with Woking ASC on the main line at Berrylands.

No 455.850 of SWT is seen at London Waterloo on 13 December 2014 in platform 4 at the head of an 8-car Kingston roundabout service. *Jason Cross*

Kew Bridge on a bright April day in 2015 sees newly repainted South West Trains unit 455.714 on the Hounslow loop service to Waterloo *Capital Transport*

Interior of a South West Trains 455 unit. *Capital Transport*

SWT refurbished class 456 456.014 leads a Hampton Court to Waterloo service leaving New Malden on 30 April 2015. *Chris Wilson*

Expanding capacity

One way of making the infrastructure capable of accommodating more passengers is to run longer trains, but why hasn't such a solution been adopted more widely already? This section examines some of the problems.

Longer trains mean longer station platforms. This lengthening is presently being undertaken by the South West Trains/Network Rail Alliance for London inner-suburban services. If the work is confined to railway land and there are no obstructions, this can be straightforward.

Overall the challenge is how best to extend the platforms to take 10-car trains, bearing in mind the practical difficulties, the likely cost, the disruption caused while the work is under way, and the time it will take. It might be noted too that there is nowadays a presumption that level crossings will be eliminated wherever possible. Feltham, for example, is a busy station in a heavily built up area and has two side platforms. Each of these is long enough to take 8-cars. At the eastern end a road bridge carries the A244 over the railway at an angle, and on one end of this there is a tight T-junction, controlled by traffic lights. At the western end a busy level crossing carries the B3377. The decision was to close the crossing.

Quite different problems are found at London Waterloo, where the extension from 8-cars to 10-cars of Platforms 1-4 has the undesirable implication of pushing the tracks further into the concourse (and not really practicable for the whole of the distance needed), or extending the platforms round a tight curve at the country end with the consequential creation of substantial platform-train stepping distances. In turn, that could require remodelling of the station throat, underbridge rebuilding and signalling changes. It is understood that a more satisfactory solution has now been found. None of this is to argue that such work is not highly desirable; it merely emphasises that even seemingly simple tasks can be a lot more difficult and expensive than is often realised.

SOUTHERN, THAMESLINK AND GATWICK

South of the river, this is a massive operation radiating from the London termini at Victoria (for the West End) and London Bridge (for the City). Together, they equate broadly to those services operated by the South Central part of Network SouthEast, back to the days of what was once the London, Brighton & South Coast Railway.

On these tracks may be added services arriving via the Thameslink connection from Farringdon, Blackfriars and origins north of London, and those from the East London line operated by London Overground (from New Cross Gate southwards). There are also residual services associated with the one time South Eastern Railway.

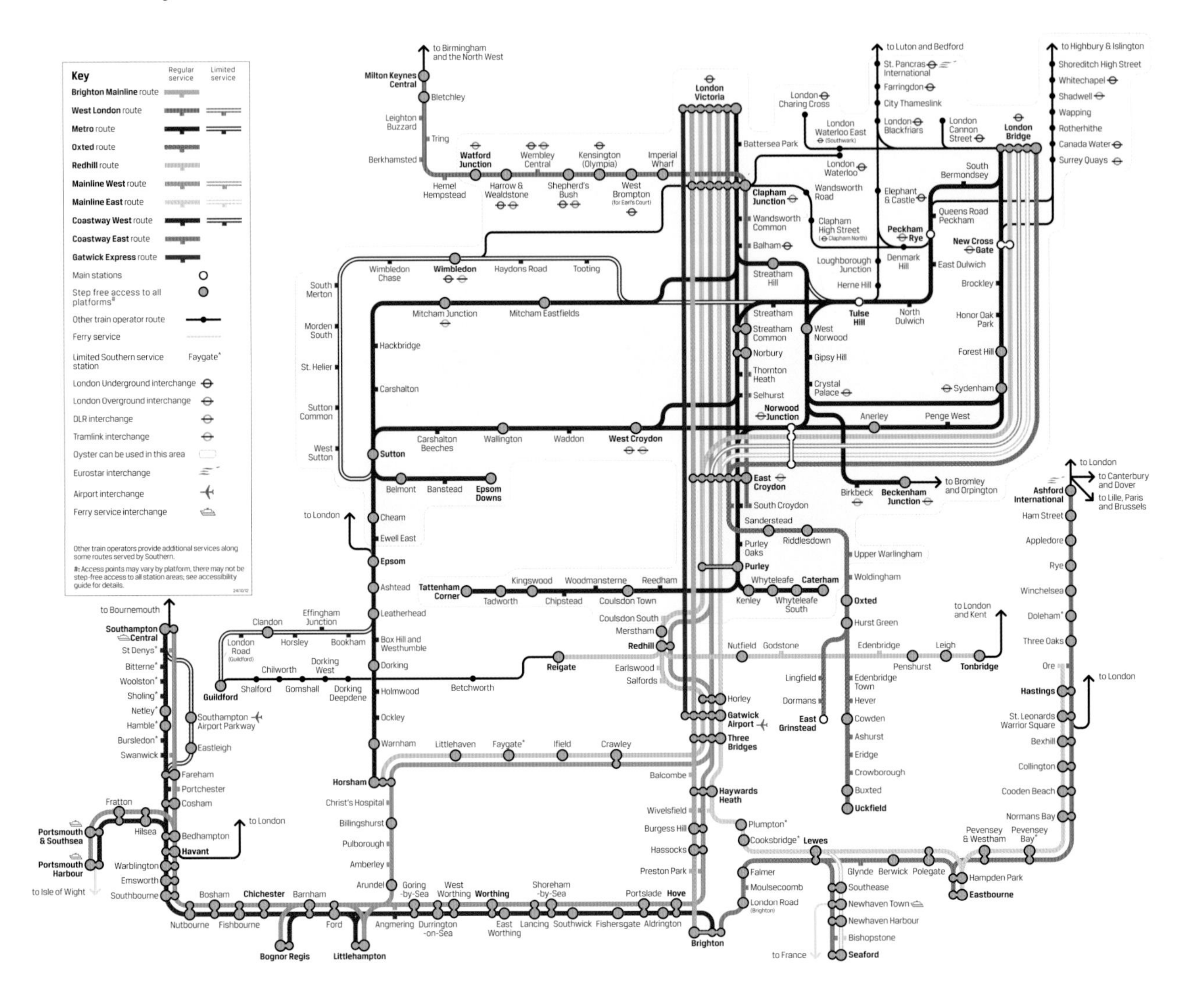

The Thameslink, Southern & Great Northern (TS&GN) franchise is all-embracing and it forms the biggest single franchise on the national railway system today. It started on 14 September 2014 and runs until September 2021. The Southern franchise, which includes Gatwick Express, ended on 26 July 2015. From that date, all Southern services were absorbed into the TS&GN franchise.

It may be of interest to reflect that at privatisation the services which are now under one management were provided by:

- Gatwick Express (London Victoria and Gatwick Airport)
- Connex South Central (Brighton main line)
- Thameslink (Bedford–Brighton via London Bridge)
- West Anglia Great Northern (services from King's Cross and Moorgate)
- Connex South Eastern (Catford Leap).

Then there were three competing companies operating between central London and Gatwick Airport; now there is only one.

455.812 heads north through Anerley on the up fast line with a train for London Bridge. The Class 455/8s were the first of three series of 455 units and were built at York between 1982 and 1984. *Kim Rennie*

The Routes

From the former London, Brighton & South Coast station at Victoria, services run to Clapham Junction and Balham. From here trains can proceed towards Crystal Palace, continuing to London Bridge via Forest Hill, to Beckenham Junction, or to Norwood Junction (and thence either East Croydon or West Croydon).

Alternatively, they can turn towards Hackbridge and Sutton, thence towards Epsom or Epsom Downs. If staying on the main line, they can run via Selhurst to East or West Croydon. East Croydon gives a whole range of Brighton main line destinations, and West Croydon a route to Sutton via Wallington.

From London Bridge, services on the Brighton lines can run via Peckham Rye, Tulse Hill and Streatham towards Hackbridge, or towards Selhurst. Also reached via Tulse Hill is Crystal Palace (and Victoria). The direct main line to Norwood Junction and both Croydon stations runs via Forest Hill.

From the central London Thameslink stations, services run via London Bridge, or via Herne Hill/Tulse and either way round the Wimbledon and Sutton loop. The main lines from both stations and thence as far as Balcombe Tunnel Junction (beyond Three Bridges) are four tracked. Some junctions are grade separated, but this is far from commonplace. The London area is controlled by Victoria and London Bridge power signalboxes. Both interface with Three Bridges PSB south of Norbury and south of Forest Hill respectively.

Services from the West Coast Main Line run via the West London Line and Clapham Junction.

With two minor exceptions, neither of which are in Greater London, the entire Southern network is electrified on the third rail 750v DC system.

The last stations on the Southern/Thameslink network in Greater London before the lines enter Surrey are Cheam, Belmont, Woodmansterne, Coulsdon South, Kenley and Riddlesdown.

The busiest stations in Greater London are Victoria (81 million), London Bridge (56m). East Croydon (22m) and Blackfriars (14m). Balham and Sutton both have around 7m passengers annually, with Denmark Hill and Peckham Rye 5m. In all cases these are the total users, so Victoria and London Bridge both include Southeastern passengers, for instance, but excludes Underground.

The London, Brighton & South Coast Railway name lives on at Clapham Junction, though the Parcels office is closed and looks as if it has been for many years. *Capital Transport*

Southern train 377.131 departs from the restored (and enhanced) Crystal Palace station for London Victoria. The centre platforms here, both single ended, were disused. They have been brought back into use to provide a terminating facility for the Overground services. *Kim Rennie*

Timetable

Essentially, the network is run on a 30-minute headway between successive trains to the same destinations, with some variations. They are shown in the pattern of departures from London Victoria, London Bridge, Shepherd's Bush, and Farringdon (for Thameslink). For services originating on the East London line, see the London Overground section.

These are the departures for the midday period, 12:00-12:59 Mondays to Fridays, which is generally repeated with minimal alterations while the off peak timetable is in operation:

Routes from Victoria - suburban

01/31 Clapham Junction, Sutton, Cheam, then alternately to Epsom and all stations except Boxhill to Dorking, or all stations via Epsom to Dorking and Horsham

03/33 all stations via Selhurst to Sutton

06/36 all stations via Crystal Palace to West Croydon and Sutton

13/43 all stations via Selhurst to Caterham

17/47 Clapham Junction, Balham, all stations via Mitcham Junction to Sutton and Epsom

19/49 all stations via Crystal Palace and Forest Hill to London Bridge

23/53 Clapham Junction and all stations via Selhurst to Sutton, then alternately to Epsom Downs and Epsom

Routes from Victoria – main line

02/32 Clapham Junction, Redhill, Gatwick Airport and stations to Horsham, dividing there alternately for Portsmouth Harbour/Bognor Regis and Southampton/Bognor Regis

06/36 Clapham Junction, East Croydon and Brighton

15/45 Gatwick Airport (non-stop)

17/47 Clapham Junction, East Croydon, Gatwick Airport, Haywards Heath, dividing there alternately for Littlehampton/Eastbourne or Littlehampton/Ore

23/53 Clapham Junction, East Croydon, Sanderstead and all stations to East Grinstead

51 Clapham Junction, East Croydon, Gatwick Airport and principal stations to Brighton

Routes from London Bridge

03/33 New Cross Gate, Norwood Junction, East Croydon, Purley and principal stations to Horsham

06/36 all stations to Caterham

08 East Croydon, Oxted and all stations to Uckfield (diesel operated)

10/40 all stations via Tulse Hill and Streatham to West Croydon

15/45 Norwood Junction, East Croydon, Purley then, alternately, all stations to Reigate and all stations to Tonbridge except Merstham

20/50 Norwood Junction, East Croydon, Purley and all stations to Tattenham Corner

22/52 all stations via Forest Hill to Crystal Palace and Victoria

25/55 all stations via Tulse Hill and Crystal Palace to Beckenham Junction

Routes from West Coast Main Line

19 ex Shepherds Bush, all stations to South Croydon

Routes from Farringdon, Thameslink

4 tph all stations to London Bridge, East Croydon, Gatwick Airport and stations to Brighton

2 tph all stations via Herne Hill and Wimbledon to Sutton

2 tph all stations via Herne Hill and Hackbridge to Sutton

2 tph all stations via Catford and Bat & Ball to Sevenoaks

Trains

The principal result of the total withdrawal of the large fleet of Mk1 electric rolling stock on Southern, now a decade ago, was a huge build of Bombardier Class 377 Electrostar units of no fewer than seven varieties. These are summarised overleaf.

New Cross Gate station on 10 June 2015 sees 377.455 with a train for London Bridge. *David Burrell*

All are leased from Porterbrook except the Class 442s, from Angel Trains. The Class 455/8s are used on the inner suburban services.

Class	Cars	Depot	No of Units	Voltage	Notes
377/1	4	Brighton	164	DC	
377/2	4	Selhurst	6	AC/DC	
377/2	4	Bedford	9	AC/DC	subleased to Thameslink
377/3	3	Selhurst	28	DC	
377/4	4	Brighton	75	DC	
377/5	4	Bedford	23	AC/DC	subleased to Thameslink
377/6	5	Selhurst	26	DC	Standard class only
377/7	5	Selhurst	8	AC/DC	Standard class only
442	5	Selhurst	24	DC	Gatwick services
455/8	4	Selhurst	46	DC	Standard class only

The Southern diesel units used for the Uckfield services (and also Ashford-Hastings) are based at Selhurst. These are Bombardier Turbostars, built in Derby from 2003. There are 10 of Class 171/7, the 2-car variety and 6 Class 171/8s of 4-cars.

A Gatwick Express train passes through Clapham Junction on its way south to the airport. *Jason Cross*

Thameslink rolling stock

The Class 319 dual-voltage fleet, which was built for Thameslink services, has already been discussed.

Bombardier is building a series of 29 4-car Class 387/1 Electrostar trains to be used on Thameslink fast services from 2015. The ROSCO is Porterbrook. These trains are intended to fill the gap between the despatch of some of the Class 319s to the new electrification in the north of England, and the arrival of the Class 700s for Thameslink which was caused by the delay in the ordering of the latter.

The Class 387/1s are dual voltage units with 110mph capability and similar generally to their Class 377 predecessors but an updated version. They have air-conditioning and are fully compliant with requirements for Persons with Reduced Mobility (PRM).

These trains are Standard class only. After the Class 700 fleet have all been delivered they will be cascaded to the electrified Great Western main line.

A further build of 27 4-car Class 387/2s will form the replacement stock for the Class 442s used on the Gatwick Express services.

For future Thameslink services, the Class 700 Siemens Desiro City trains will operate all services and are discussed later.

Other operators

At present there are other service operators in the area north of the Thames. These are Virgin Trains East Coast (London King's Cross to North/North East England), Hull Trains and Grand Central (open access operators), and East Midland Trains (London St Pancras to the East Midlands). Freight is of modest impact.

South of the Thames, there are interfaces with South West Trains, Southeastern and London Overground. Domestic operations on High Speed 1 do not impinge on the London area, nor do First Great Western services between Reading and Gatwick Airport.

The interior of a Class 319 Thameslink train with 3+2 seating was photographed in June 2015. Even allowing for the age of these units, the interior is at best austere, and the general apparent glumness of the passengers somehow seems to fit. *Capital Transport*

Future Thameslink

The success of the initial Thameslink reconstruction and upgrade was only partial, in that it was just not possible to provide adequate line capacity to meet growing traffic levels.

The result was the Thameslink programme, requiring major expansions of the infrastructure and, eventually, just about everything else. The original Thameslink 2000 title was quietly dropped many years ago. It is scheduled that this very extensive upgrade, with new trains, will be in full operation from December 2018.

The principal aim is the establishment of a reliable 24 tph capacity through the Thameslink central core between St Pancras low level and Blackfriars. This is the key determinant of what service levels can be provided for the travelling public. Of those 24 trains through Blackfriars, 16 are intended to proceed via London Bridge, with the remaining 8 running via Elephant & Castle.

Thameslink programme

This is a large scale programme costing £6.5bn of which £4.5bn is for infrastructure works. The main works (some of which are now complete) include:

- Rebuilding Blackfriars station, with pedestrian entrances on both sides of the River Thames;
- The rebuilding of Farringdon station, to include interchange with the forthcoming Crossrail. This will then become the London station with direct services to each of Heathrow, Gatwick and Luton Airports;
- Construction of a new low level station at St Pancras International to replace the earlier King's Cross Thameslink platforms;
- The building of a connection from St Pancras International, which includes the construction of the new Canal Tunnels to the Great Northern lines out of London King's Cross at a point between Gasworks and Copenhagen tunnels;
- Platform lengthening to 12-cars in much of the area served, which can involve substantial works in terms of bridge rebuilding and similar;
- Power supply upgrades to meet increased traction demands;
- Construction of new maintenance depots at Hornsey and Three Bridges and the extension of stabling sites elsewhere;
- Fitting out the new works generally;
- Substantial resignalling, including the installation of the European Train Control System (ETCS) and Automatic Train Operation (ATO) in the core area;
- London Bridge station area rebuilding.

London Bridge station

The complete rebuilding of London Bridge station is a major task in its own right. This includes its approaches from various directions, and is a major determinant of both the feasibility and construction timescale of a vastly expanded Thameslink service.

Briefly, this work consists of building a huge new low level concourse with direct access to all platforms, the rearrangement of tracks to separate out the various groups of services as far as possible, two new tracks and new platforms to cater for trains to and from Charing Cross, and building the Bermondsey diveunder to obviate movements in which the train paths for Thameslink and Southeastern services conflict with each other.

This requires the progressive closure of the various parts of the station, starting with the terminating platforms on the Brighton side (old numbers 10-16). This Stage 1 work is now largely complete, with the central core of the station now being tackled (essentially the Charing Cross and Blackfriars (for Thameslink) lines. Stage 2 is taking place over the whole of 2015 and to August 2016.

The last section to be rebuilt (August 2016 to 2018) will be the northernmost part, used by Cannon Street services.

Thameslink trains

The new Class 700 Desiro City trains ordered from Siemens are around 25% lighter than their Class 319 predecessors, thanks to features such as new bogie design with inboard bearings, lower energy consumption, decreased wheel and track wear damage, and the maintenance costs of both. The trains will be air-conditioned, have an integrated Driver Advisory System (DAS), and LED lighting.

The contract requires the construction of a total of 1,140 vehicles to form 115 trains. They are of two varieties; the Class 700/0 8-car formation of which 60 are being built and 55 of Class 700/1, a 12-car variant. They are being financed by the Cross London Trains consortium.

These Desiro City trains will be brought into service progressively from 2016, with the full 24 tph service through Blackfriars from 2018. Siemens is also responsible for train maintenance at the two new depots that the company is building at Three Bridges (Brighton line) and Hornsey (GN).

These vehicles are of a nominal 20 metres in length. Accommodation will be mostly Standard class, with First Class seats situated in the Driving Motor Cars at the extreme ends of the sets. Top speed is 100mph.

The trains will not be divisible in normal service and will run singly, with internal gangways from end to end. This obviates the provision of intermediate driving cabs, meaning that this space can be used for passengers instead. On the other hand, even an 8-car unit will require a station platform length of 160 metres or so if all the train doors are to be used.

The Class 700 trains will be dual voltage units, for which the changeover between AC and DC will take place, as now, while stationary at Farringdon.

They will not be able to venture onto the route from Finsbury Park to Moorgate. This carries the GN inner suburban services from Welwyn Garden City (20 miles from central London) or Hertford North (21 miles). Apart from anything else, six-car operation (presently with Class 313/0s) is the maximum train length possible.

The Thameslink class 700 Desiro City stock is scheduled to begin service in 2016. *Siemens*

Interim arrangements

Works which affect the running of the Southern services which terminate at London Bridge (the high numbered platforms 10-15) were effectively completed at the end of 2014.

Attention then turned to the rest of the station and Platforms 1-9 (new numbers). Of these, Platforms 1-3 are for Cannon Street services, the island Platforms 4-5 for Thameslink, island platform 6-7 (loop) for down Charing Cross services and island platform 8-9 (loop) for up Charing Cross trains.

There are major service changes and the following is a general guide. There will be other short term changes.

January 2015 to January 2018:

- All Bedford–Brighton cross-London Thameslink services run via Elephant & Castle, avoiding London Bridge.
- A reduced Thameslink off-peak Monday to Saturday service runs between Brighton and London Bridge and a very limited service runs in the peak.

January 2015 to August 2016

- Southeastern services to Charing Cross do not stop at London Bridge.
- Southeastern services between Charing Cross and Woolwich Dockyard, Plumstead, Belvedere and Erith are diverted to Cannon Street.
- Southeastern Cannon Street services continue to stop at London Bridge.
- Some diversions are taking place between Charing Cross, Cannon Street and Blackfriars.

January 2015 onwards

- Southeastern services to or from New Cross, St John's, Deptford, Greenwich, Maze Hill and Westcombe Park are diverted to Cannon Street. These stations have no Charing Cross services and the change is permanent.

August 2016 to January 2018

- Southeastern services to and from Charing Cross resume calling at London Bridge.
- Southeastern services to and from Cannon Street will not call at London Bridge. Some diversions will take place between Charing Cross, Cannon Street and Blackfriars.

2018

- Cannon Street services resume calling at London Bridge.
- Thameslink route services resume calling at London Bridge.
- Completion of track, signalling and major bridge work around London Bridge station.
- Expanded Thameslink service introduced.

Ultimate service patterns

One result of this is a certain imbalance in the Thameslink service pattern in the proposed 2018 timetable.

North of the Thames, destinations are mainly in the outer-suburban category. These include places such as Bedford (50 miles from central London), Peterborough (76 miles) and Cambridge (58 miles). Luton (30 miles) is closer.

South of the Thames the situation is very different; apart from Brighton (51 miles) and perhaps Horsham (35 miles), other destinations pencilled in for all day services are Gatwick Airport (27 miles), Sevenoaks (27 miles) and the modestly used branch to Tattenham Corner (22 miles). This might be handy for attending the Derby at Epsom, but that is only one day a year.

In addition, it is intended that the trains on the Wimbledon/Sutton loop will continue north of Blackfriars (rather than terminating there), and run to St Albans (20 miles).

A number of additional services to a greater variety of destinations are (e.g. Maidstone East, supplementing Southeastern services) to be run during the peak hours.

This range of operations, it would seem, will be serving a variety of markets, with only two types of train to satisfy passenger demands.

The Integrated Kent mini-franchise is operated by GoVia, trading as Southeastern. It began on 21 December 2014 and runs until June 2018.

Like other services on the third rail network, Southeastern services can be divided into inner and outer destinations. The company also have City and West End termini.

Southeastern operate from Charing Cross and Cannon Street (former South Eastern Railway services), Victoria and Blackfriars (former London, Chatham & Dover Railway services). These were originally largely separate networks, resulting in a complex series of routes and connections between them. Southeastern also operate domestic services on HS1 from London St Pancras to Kent, but these are outside the scope of this book.

The busiest stations for Southeastern are Charing Cross with 40 million passengers a year, Cannon Street with 21m, Lewisham 9m, Waterloo East 7m, with Bromley South and Orpington at 7m.

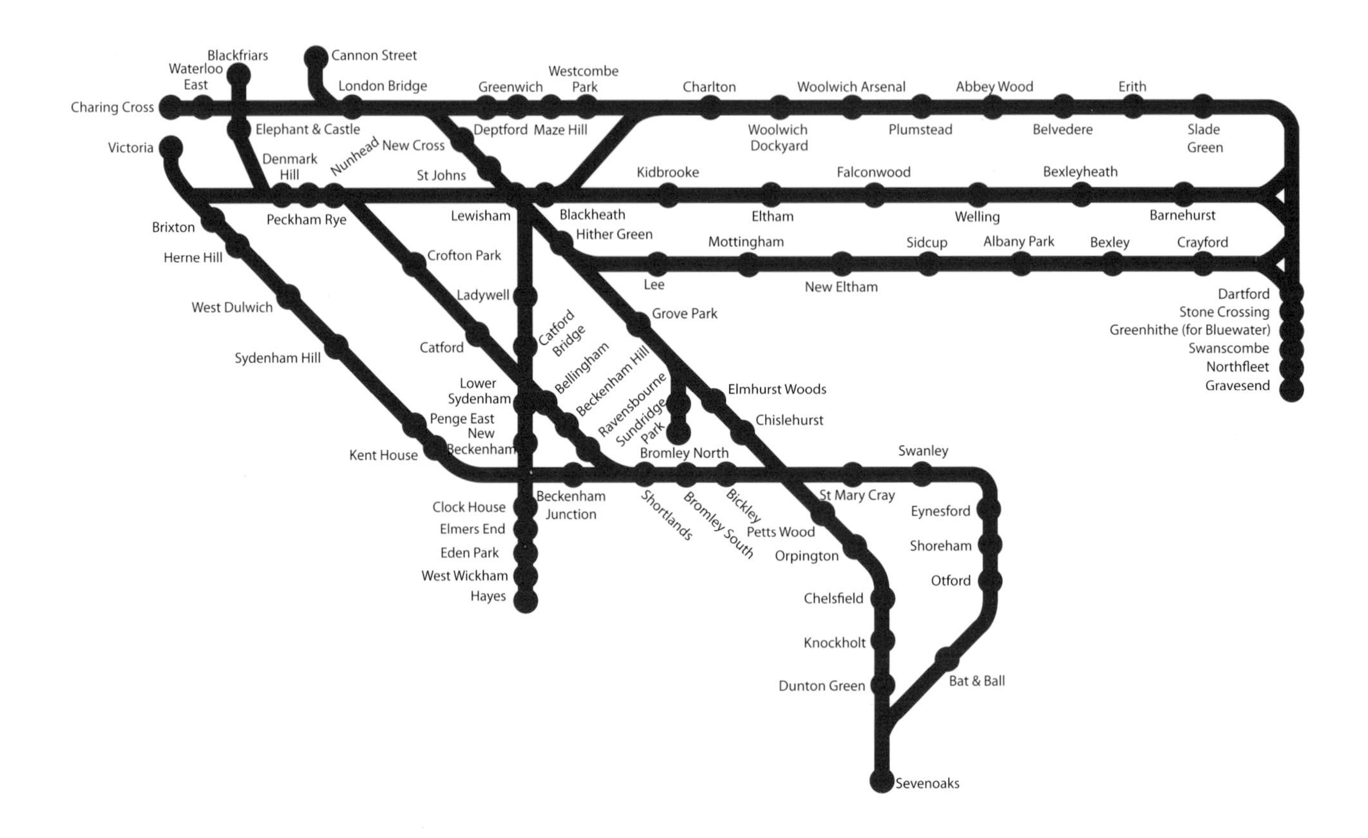

No 376 010 approaches Waterloo East with a wide variety of architectural styles in the background, from a 1960s box to The Shard.
Capital Transport

Routes

On the Southeastern side, the four track main line east of London Bridge continues to Orpington, where it reduces to two tracks. In the process it throws off branches to each of the three North Kent lines to Dartford (via Maze Hill, Sidcup and Eltham respectively), for Hayes and for Bromley North. Beyond Chislehurst it crosses above the Chatham main line from Victoria, with which it makes numerous connections.

From Victoria, the double tracked route is via Brixton to Beckenham Junction, and Shortlands. Here it joins the alternative route from Victoria via Peckham Rye and Catford. There are four tracks through Bromley South and under the South Eastern as far as Swanley. Trains can continue to Chatham, Faversham and East Kent, or leave the main line here to reach Sevenoaks and the line via Maidstone East.

The last stations on Southeastern in Greater London before trains enter Kent are Knockholt, St Mary Cray, Crayford, Barnehurst and Slade Green.

The ornate station building on the bridge over Denmark Hill station is partly visible in this view of a Southeastern train on a Victoria service formed from unit 465.152. *Kim Rennie*

The Timetable

Routes from Charing Cross; all services call at Waterloo East

00/30 Orpington, Sevenoaks and stations to Tunbridge Wells
02/32 Lewisham and all stations via Eltham to Dartford
06/36 Hither Green and all stations to Sevenoaks
09/39 Lewisham, Blackheath, Woolwich Arsenal and principal stations to Gillingham
10/40 Sevenoaks, Tonbridge and stations to Ashford International, dividing there for routes towards Canterbury West or Dover Priory
15/45 Orpington, Sevenoaks, Tonbridge and stations to Hastings
17/47 Ladywell and all stations to Hayes
26/56 All stations via Sidcup to Dartford and Gravesend

Additionally, a connecting shuttle service runs at 15/35/55 between Grove Park, Sundridge Park and Bromley North

Routes from Cannon Street; all services call at London Bridge

00/30 All stations to Hayes
07/17/27/37/47/57 All stations via Maze Hill to Slade Green, of which 2tph extended to Dartford
10/40 All stations to Crayford, continuing to Charlton via Dartford loop and then back to Cannon Street.
20/50 All stations to Orpington
24/54 All stations via Eltham to Slade Green

Routes from Victoria, Chatham side

07/37 Bromley South, Swanley, Otford and principal stations via Maidstone East to Ashford International, alternately Bromley South and all stations to Ashford International
09/39 Denmark Hill, Peckham Rye, Nunhead, Lewisham and all stations via Eltham to Dartford
10/25/40/55 All stations via Herne Hill to Orpington
22/52 Bromley South, stations to Faversham, dividing there for Margate or Dover Priory
58 Bromley South, all stations to Gillingham

Southeastern services stopping at London Bridge have had to be reduced substantially while the Thameslink programme is under way. At Borough Market junction, a new connection has been built that will receive track to accommodate Thameslink trains from 2018. *Capital Transport*

Trains

South Eastern services are operated by a fleet of Class 375/376 Electrostars built by Bombardier at Derby between 1999 and 2005, and a series of Class 465 Networkers from British Rail days for inner-suburban work. These date from 1991-93. Classes 465/0 and 465/1 were built by BREL at York, the remainder by Metro-Cammell. The whole fleet is 1st/Standard class, unless noted otherwise.

There are also the 29 Hitachi Class 395s used on HS1 services, which do not concern us here.

Class	Cars	Depot	Units	Voltage	Notes
375/3	3	Ramsgate	10	DC	express units
375/6	4	Ramsgate	30	DC/AC	express units
375/7	4	Ramsgate	15	DC	express units
375/8	4	Ramsgate	30	DC	express units
375/9	4	Ramsgate	27	DC	outer suburban
376	5	Slade Green	36	DC	inner suburban, standard class
465/0	4	Slade Green	50	DC	Standard class
465/1	4	Slade Green	47	DC	Standard class
465/2	4	Slade Green	16*	DC	Standard class
465/9	4	Slade Green	34*	DC	1st/Standard
466	2	Slade Green	43*	DC	Standard

All are leased from Eversholt except those marked * which are leased from Angel Trains.

Control

Control in the London area is by London Bridge Area Signalling Centre (ASC), which interfaces with Ashford beyond various points on the North Kent lines and at Grove Park. Victoria ASC controls the various routes to and beyond Bromley South.

In June 2015 South Eastern's 465.168 is arriving at Shortlands. *Capital Transport*

Interior of a 465 unit of the type used on London suburban services. *Capital Transport*

Interior of a 376, units of which are principally used on services into Cannon Street. *Capital Transport*

London Overground is operated as a concession managed by Transport for London.

Concessions are a form of management contract. The awarding body takes the decisions on the level of service to be provided, operating hours, staffing levels and the fares be charged. It is also responsible for investment in the system and the trains.

The concession holder runs the train services and stations within defined quality parameters, providing the customer service and operations staff. The infrastructure remains the responsibility of Network Rail.

The London Overground concession has been operated by MTR and Arriva Trains (DB) trading as LOROL (London Rail Operations Ltd) since 11 November 2007. This contract continues until November 2016. It was awarded and managed by TfL subsidiary Rail for London Ltd and from 31 May 2015 it included what were formerly West Anglia services to Cheshunt, Enfield Town and Chingford, also Romford–Upminster (see later).

At the contract's termination, London Overground services will be retendered as a whole.

Capitalstar 378.255 leaves South Acton with a Stratford to Richmond train. Behind the station building on the other platform was once the terminus of the single track District line branch from Acton Town, abandoned in 1959 and now completely obliterated.
Capital Transport

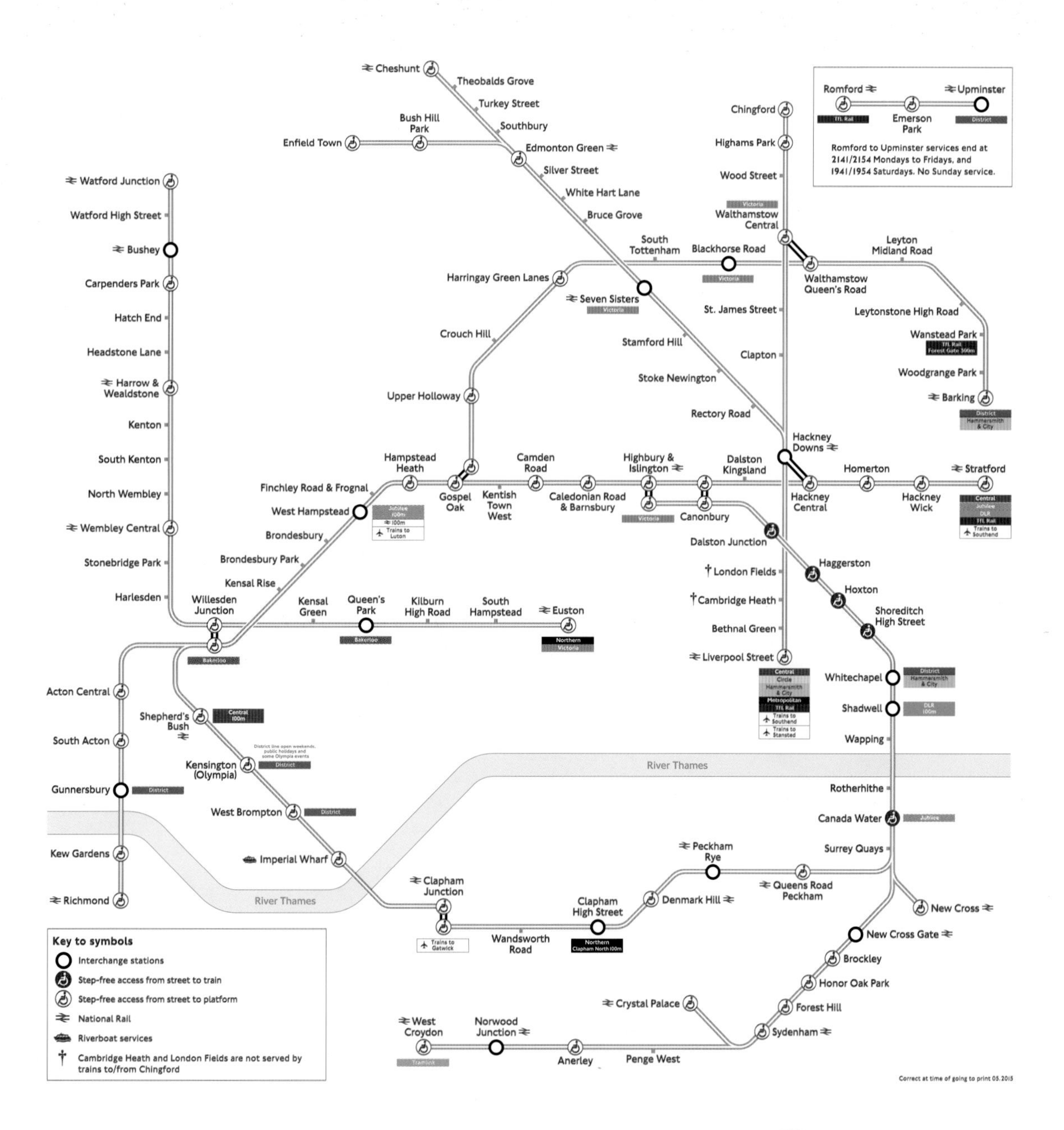

MAYOR OF LONDON

Train services

The original London Overground network as introduced in 2007 consists of five elements, with the names by which they have been known generally in brackets. All trains on these lines call at all stations and the basic service level is 4 tph on electrified services.

- Richmond to Willesden Junction, Gospel Oak, Highbury & Islington and Stratford (the North London Line).
- Clapham Junction to Willesden Junction (the West London Line). Alternate trains are extended via Gospel Oak and Highbury & Islington to Stratford, thus providing an irregular 6 tph over this section.
- Dalston Junction to Surrey Quays (the East London Line). This core section carries four different services, each at 4 tph, making 16 tph through the tunnel under the Thames between Wapping and Rotherhithe. These services are:

  Dalston Junction and New Cross
  Highbury & Islington and Clapham Junction (via Peckham Rye)
  Dalston Junction and West Croydon
  Highbury & Islington and Crystal Palace.

Together, these routes offer 8 tph between Highbury & Islington and Dalston Junction and 8 tph also on the section between Surrey Quays and Sydenham, where Crystal Palace services branch off from those to West Croydon.

- Euston to Willesden Junction and Watford Junction (the DC lines). These services have a basic frequency of 3 tph, but they are supplemented by London Underground Bakerloo line services between Queen's Park and Harrow & Wealdstone. Stations north of Hatch End are in Hertfordshire.
- Gospel Oak to Barking (the Tottenham & Hampstead line). The core services here run at 4 tph.

The scene is Platforms 5 and 6 at Richmond, a South West Trains station, with London Overground unit 378.223 on 13 October 2013, The tracks at platforms 4 to 7 have fourth rail dc electrification, since their use is shared with the District line of London Underground. *Jason Cross*

Electrification

The 25kV AC overhead electrification extends from Acton Central station platforms to Stratford, and also from Willesden Junction to a little beyond North Pole Junction on the West London Line. The main lines out of London Euston are also 25kV AC, but these are in effect completely separate from the DC lines alongside.

The 750v DC third rail extends from London Euston to Watford Junction, with a section of 4th rail DC between Queen's Park and Harrow & Wealdstone to accommodate the Bakerloo trains.

The East London Line from Highbury & Islington to the four destinations of New Cross, West Croydon, Crystal Palace and Clapham Junction (Platform 2) is entirely third rail. Also third rail is the line from Acton Central to Richmond (but with 4th rail for sharing with London Underground District line trains between Gunnersbury and Richmond) and the West London line section from North Pole to Clapham Junction station (Platform 1).

It has been announced that the Tottenham & Hampstead line is to be electrified at 25kV AC. Included in this project is the increase of overhead clearances at 29 overbridges, of which two need complete reconstruction. At present short sections of AC exist at South Tottenham and between Woodgrange Park Junction and Barking, but are of no consequence for these passenger operations.

Both 3rd and 4th rail DC trains can use track equipped with a 3rd rail only. The electrical current is returned via the running rails rather than the centre 4th rail, a practice established many years ago. However, movements which require a change between AC and DC traction require the use of dual voltage trains. The result for London Overground has been the creation of two separate fleets.

The Class 378/1 fleet of 20 trains is DC only, the Class 378/2 fleet of 37 trains has AC/DC capability. Both fleets are otherwise all but identical, and the conversion of all or part of the DC only fleet to AC/DC would be a relatively simple matter.

London Overground dual voltage unit 378.220 arrives at Hackney Wick in May 2015, an area with much potential for redevelopment made more likely with the recent improvements to the railway service following takeover by TfL. *Capital Transport*

Trains

The original Class 378 trains were built by Bombardier at Derby from 2008 and are known as Capitalstars. Early versions of the Class 378/2s were built as 3-car units, extended to 4-cars in 2010. The Class 378/1 units were built as 4-cars from the outset. Further extension for the whole fleet to 5-cars is taking place for trains on the East London lines, to be followed by the Richmond/Clapham Junction–Stratford services by the end of 2015.

All are air-conditioned and were built with two novel features (for National Railways). First, there are wide gangways between adjacent vehicles. This seems to be popular with passengers as it allows easy movement within a train and is perceived as having security benefits.

Second, seating is wholly longitudinal at around 36 seats in each car. This is not many seats for 20 metre vehicles, which with a conventional 3+2 layout might be expected to accommodate twice that number of seats. However, it does give that much more standing room and many journeys on these services by passengers are relatively short. There are two sets of double sliding doors on each side of each car.

Introduction of longer trains has required modifications such as platform extensions, a programme which was largely completed during 2014. Where rebuilding is impractical, recourse is having to be made to Selective Door Opening, whereby the last set of doors in a train are not opened. This is the case at Wapping, Rotherhithe and at Canada Water (a station which was opened only in 1999). Until such time as Crossrail works are finished, the same situation arises at Whitechapel. Such situations are not ideal and can result in extended station stop times.

Other requirements are changes to signalling and extensions to facilities such as maintenance areas, turnback sidings and depot stabling. The primary maintenance and stabling depot for electric trains is at New Cross Gate, supplemented by Willesden Junction. New stabling facilities have been built at Silwood (near New Cross Gate depot) and are under construction at Wembley (within the Wembley European Freight Operating Centre near Stonebridge Park).

The Class 378s are supplied to Transport for London by QW Rail Leasing.

The new Overground station at Dalston Junction. *Capital Transport*

Inside a 378 unit. Nice though the interiors and seats are, they bring with them an absence of the more popular transverse seating.

Gospel Oak–Barking

These services are run at present with a fleet of eight Class 172/0 Turbostar 2-car units built by Bombardier at Derby from 2009. They are maintained at Willesden TMD and have conventional transverse seating. They are leased from Angel Trains.

Electrification will require additional fleet and the adjustment of stabling and maintenance facilities. It will also enable service revisions to take place, notably the potential for the extension of services from Barking to new destinations west of Gospel Oak. That does however raise some questions about train calls at Gospel Oak station itself, and how a second platform might be accommodated.

Interchange opportunities on the London Overground group of lines is not all it might be, given the lengths of route covered. The Gospel Oak-Barking line is particularly poor; the only true rail interchange other than at the termini is at Blackhorse Road, where the station premises are now shared with the Victoria line of London Underground. Attempts are now being made to popularise the link from Walthamstow Queen's Road and Walthamstow Central, a five-minute walk.

On 28 September 2013, diesel unit no 172.004 arrives at Gospel Oak, with a train from Barking. Electrification will see the use of longer trains on this line. The tracks on the left link the Tottenham & Hampstead line with the North London and are likely to be brought into passenger use as and when electrification takes place. *Chris Wilson*

Great Eastern

So much for the core London Overground operation. 31 May 2015 saw the responsibility for the procurement and operation of most north east London Liverpool Street services transferred from the Department for Transport to Transport for London. Previously, they were part of the Greater Anglia franchise. This consists of the following basic all stations services:

- 4 tph Liverpool Street–Chingford
- 2 tph Liverpool Street–Enfield Town
- 2 tph Liverpool Street–Cheshunt via Seven Sisters

The section between Liverpool Street and Edmonton Green, where the Enfield and Cheshunt lines diverge, receives 4 tph due to services overlapping.

All are now part of London Overground but remain running on part of the National Rail system.

A further addition was the isolated short branch between Romford and Upminster with its single intermediate station of Emerson Park (2 tph). This is a feeder to the emerging Crossrail operation.

All these services are operated by the present ageing Class 315 units dating from 1980. New rolling stock will be provided and an additional eight will be required for the newly electrified Gospel Oak–Barking service and one for Romford–Upminster. They are to be supplied by 2017/18.

In the meantime, TfL are sprucing up the Class 315s. Improvements are also promised for the stations to be served. All 23 will form part of an extended London Overground, except for Liverpool Street (Network Rail), Cheshunt (remaining with Abellio), Romford (Crossrail) and Upminster (c2c). Both Theobalds Grove and Cheshunt stations are in Hertfordshire.

Apart from Liverpool Street itself, there are important interchanges with London Underground at Seven Sisters and Walthamstow Central.

Fourteen 317s were transferred to London Overground from Abellio in May 2015. The Great Eastern services are also worked by 315s transferred from Abellio.

The majority of the services taken over from Abellio in May 2015 are worked by 315 units, one of which is seen in full Overground livery at Chingford. The station name signs were initially covered with vinyls for the new operator, Enfield Town being the first to receive new enamel signage. *Capital Transport*

Inside a refurbished 315 car, showing use of the same moquette seat covering as on the new-build Overground trains. *Capital Transport*

Car 317 64494 has been fitted with a nameplate for TfL. It is part of the formation of 315.817, which was the first unit to be refurbished by TfL.

Timetable

The off peak timetable Mondays to Fridays offers 4 tph from Liverpool Street to Chingford, 2 tph to Enfield Town and 2 tph to Cheshunt via Southbury. These trains call at all stations, though the Chingford trains do not stop at Cambridge Heath or London Fields.

During the Monday to Friday evening peak from 17:00 to 17:59, the Chingford and Cheshunt stopping services stay much the same, but Enfield Town services are increased to 4 tph.

On Saturdays and Sundays the Chingford and Enfield Town services are the same as the Monday to Friday off peak; the Cheshunt services become limited stop on the section to Edmonton Green.

Romford–Upminster shuttles run twice an hour on weekdays only; there is no Sunday service.

Trains

Trains are formed using the 61 sets of Class 315 4-car units, built at York in 1981. All are 20m vehicles of Standard Class only; they are maintained at Ilford and leased from Eversholt ROSCO. As built they seat 298 in 3+2 facing pairs, though many have one vehicle adapted to carry wheelchairs. There are no toilets.

Further Overground extension?

A further proposal is the extension of the service from Gospel Oak beyond Barking to Barking Riverside, a distance of about 4km. This is in connection with the construction of up to 10,800 new homes (for which planning permission has been given) as well as community facilities.

This service would cease to use the present terminal Platform 1 at Barking and instead continue over the existing flyover from Barking Station Junction to reach the Tilbury line Platforms 7 and 8. Trains would continue on the Tilbury line towards Dagenham Dock for about two miles, but then make a sharp turn over new construction to the south, shortly after passing under Renwick Road bridge.

This would be a new section of railway built on a viaduct, about one mile in length, to a new Barking Riverside station. This would be located in the heart of a new district centre.

Earlier proposals of a Docklands Light Railway extension to this area have been discarded.

Initial consultation on this proposal was undertaken in autumn 2014. Subject to funding, further consultation and endorsement by the Mayor, it is intended to submit an application for a Transport & Works Act Order. This might be lodged by the end of 2015. Quite how this additional use by passenger services would fit in with the expanding freight traffic to and from the new London Gateway port on the Thames Haven branch is something which will have to be determined.

If approved, construction of the extension could start in early 2017, with opening at the end of 2019.

By then, according to TfL, the Gospel Oak–Barking line itself will have been electrified.

Usage

Of the stations served mainly or exclusively by London Overground as a National Rail service, the busiest are Camden Road, Canada Water, Dalston Kingsland, Forest Hill, Hackney Central, Homerton and Kensington Olympia. All have around 6m to 7m passenger entries and exits a year.

TfL Rail is the trading name for what are being called the Great Eastern Metro services, that is the stopping services between London Liverpool Street and Shenfield. They are, in fact, those that made up the original DC electrification to Shenfield of 1949.

On 31 May 2015 these services were transferred from Abellio Greater Anglia to TfL and the appointed operator of both trains and stations, MTR Crossrail Ltd. TfL is responsible for ensuring that the services operate in accordance with the concession agreement. The infrastructure remains the responsibility of Network Rail.

Thus TfL sets the specifications for train frequency, sets standards for station facilities and overall performance, and manages fares and revenue. TfL also plans and funds improvements.

In the short term, TfL:

- will ensure that there are staff on duty at every station from first to last trains
- will provide cleaner trains and deep clean the stations
- will improve customer information
- will tackle fare evasion and anti-social behaviour
- will improve service integration into the rest of the public transport network, and
- have committed themselves to improving reliability.

In the long term, TfL will work to improve service standards and introduce the new Class 345 trains presently under construction from May 2017.

In May 2019 Crossrail services will start to run between Shenfield and Paddington, to be extended beyond to Heathrow Terminal 4 and to Reading in December 2019. It is likely though that some peak services will still run between Shenfield and London Liverpool Street main line terminal, as they do at present.

TfL Rail has just one line, the Liverpool Street to Shenfield service for which it has become responsible pending the opening of Crossrail. The now rather elderly trains are receiving this new livery and new seat covering. *Kim Rennie*

The initial Crossrail scheme is to operate from Shenfield and Abbey Wood in the west to Heathrow Airport and Reading in the east.

The Crossrail concept is the linking of existing railways on opposite sides of London via a new deep level line through the centre of the capital. In the process, this provides much increased rail capacity overall, eases pressures on the distribution of those arriving by rail at the London termini concerned (mostly the Underground or buses), and for many users reduces, or eliminates, the need to change trains in the course of their overall journeys.

Route

The route chosen was from Shenfield on the existing Great Eastern line and serves all the present stations using the Electric (Slow) Line tracks to Stratford. It enters a new tunnel at Pudding Mill Lane portal, leading to the underground junction in the vicinity of Stepney Green.

The route from the existing but enlarged Southeastern surface station at Abbey Wood quickly goes underground to a new station at Woolwich. It continues beneath the Thames; after a short surface section it then drops again to use the Connaught Tunnel under the docks, before rising to the surface and the completely rebuilt station of Custom House. This section is built on the formation of what was once the North Woolwich branch of the Great Eastern Railway. On leaving Custom House, the line enters tunnel again, with the next station at Canary Wharf and on to Stepney Green.

The combined railway then has new underground stations at Whitechapel, Liverpool Street, Farringdon, Bond Street and Paddington.

West of Paddington, the line rises to the surface at the Royal Oak portal and takes the Relief Lines thence to Reading, serving all the existing stations and the branch to Heathrow.

Crossrail will serve a total of 40 stations.

Construction

Following many years of preparation, the Crossrail Act received Royal Assent on 22 July 2008. This is a £14.5bn scheme, with an additional £1bn requirement for the rolling stock.

The construction of this 118km railway began in 2009 and is expected to be in full operation in 2019. The pre-existing infrastructure will belong to Network Rail. That is the section east of the Pudding Mill Lane portal and west of the Royal Oak portal. The Abbey Wood branch does not run over tracks which were previously part of the national railway system.

The central section is wholly in tunnel. The major civils construction work consists of tunnelling, both for the pairs of broadly parallel running tunnels and the much enlarged tunnels for the underground stations.

Most of the Tunnel Boring Machines (TBMs) were of the earth pressure balance type, but those for the Plumstead-North Woolwich section, Mary and Sophia, were slurry based to cope with the rather different ground conditions south of the river.

The first tunnel drive to be completed was that by the TBM Phyllis. Work started from Royal Oak on 3 May 2012 and Phyllis arrived at Farringdon on 7 October 2013.

These are single bore tunnels totalling 21km in length, making 42km of excavation in all. This has required the use of eight TBMs, one for each drive. Two of these made two bores each. The five tunnelled sections are detailed in the table on page 57.

Opposite: Canary Wharf Crossrail station at an advanced stage of construction in May 2015. *Capital Transport*

Crossrail tunnel sections

Km	Section	Direction	TBM	Complete
6.4km	Royal Oak to Farringdon	Eastbound	Ada	27 01 14
6.4km	Royal Oak to Farringdon	Westbound	Phyllis	07 12 13
8.3km	Limmo Peninsula to Farringdon	Eastbound	Elizabeth	11 05 15
8.3km	Limmo Peninsula to Farringdon	Westbound	Victoria	26 05 15
2.7km	Pudding Mill Lane to Stepney Green	Eastbound	Jessica	03 02 14
2.7km	Pudding Mill Lane to Stepney Green	Westbound	Ellie	13 06 14
0.9km	Limmo Peninsula to Victoria Dock	Eastbound	Ellie	18 10 14
0.9km	Limmo Peninsula to Victoria Dock	Westbound	Jessica	05 08 14
0.6km	Connaught Tunnel (existing)	Reconstruction work		29 07 14
2.6km	Plumstead to North Woolwich	Eastbound	Mary	22 05 14
2.6km	Plumstead to North Woolwich	Westbound	Sophia	29 01 14

Between the totally rebuilt Custom House station and the former Silvertown station, the double track Connaught Tunnel was used by the North Woolwich branch trains until their withdrawal on 10 December 2006. This has been reconstructed for Crossrail use and takes the new railway below the shipping link between the Royal Victoria and Royal Albert docks.

The new tunnels have had to slot in between existing subsurface tunnels for various purposes (not just those for other railways) and clearances could be very tight. When TBM Phyllis passed above the Northern Line tunnels at Tottenham Court Road, there was a mere 853mm to spare. It was also necessary to route the tunnelling clear of the boxes needed for the Crossrail escalators.

Tunnel lining is by concrete rings. A single ring consists of eight concrete pieces, which were cast in purpose built facilities at either Old Oak Common or Chatham. To give an idea of the scale of this work, 250,000 separate tunnel rings were needed in total. Each work team might instal around 20 rings a day.

Within the site, narrow gauge railways have been used for the movement of spoil from the Tunnel Boring Machines, and also to transport staff to and from the underground workfaces.

Another aspect was the removal of spoil. Sidings at Westbourne Park saw 860 train loads moved by GB Railfreight. These were taken to Northfleet then by barge as part of a plan to build up the RSPB centre of Wallasea Island in the Thames Estuary. This was part of the 4.5m tonnes being moved in total.

The TBMs are large pieces of equipment, around 148 metres in length. Their final disposal was usually to bury the front end in a side tunnel built for the purpose, then dismantle the pieces at the back for reuse.

Next stage

Large diameter but empty tunnels are of little use on their own. With the completion of the tunnelling work in 2015, the emphasis turns to the fitting out of the newly created infrastructure. This includes track laying, the provision of power supply, installation of overhead equipment, the design, installation and commissioning of the signalling and train control equipment, the completion of the stations and communication systems.

The scale of the stations work can be judged by the new Canary Wharf station, which includes provision for leisure activities and a shopping centre. There will be three levels of stores, restaurants and gyms, with a park on the top floor. The retail side opened in 2015, three years before Crossrail trains are running below. When complete, this complex will include 17 escalators and 6 lifts. Its extent is expected to rival that of St Pancras International.

There is only one completely new Crossrail station above ground and that is at Custom House, where interchange will be available with the DLR. This is on the old station site, of which nothing remains.

A total of 41km of overhead conductor rails (i.e. fixed in position rather than suspended wires) will be installed; also power, ventilation, drainage and fire prevention/emergency provision systems. There are to be 48 ventilation fans, 40km of walkways, 66 drainage pumps and 40km of fire mains. All running tunnels will be lit throughout.

Separately, there are the links to the existing railways. Physical links are being made at each end of the central section, but there are requirements for passenger interchange with London Underground lines, London Overground lines, National Rail or the Docklands Light Railway as well.

Crossrail stations on the central section feature interchange with one or more other railway service providers. In itself this is a cause of major reconstructions, to cope with the large increase of passenger traffic at these locations, to which needs to be added those merely requiring street access to and from Crossrail services.

Network Rail

Network Rail are responsible for the reconstruction or improvement of 27 stations, 61km of track, 179 points and crossings, the upgrading of the existing signalling and around 1,000 overhead electrification structures.

For Crossrail, new station buildings are being provided at Acton Main Line, West Ealing, Southall and Hayes & Harlington.

There are major station reconstruction works at Ealing Broadway. The provision of lifts and platform extensions are needed at West Drayton and Maidenhead, plus a new Platform 6 at Maidenhead. Platform extensions are required at Iver, Langley, Slough and Burnham. Electrification has to be provided west of Airport Junction to Reading (and indeed to Bristol and South Wales). Stockley flyover has been rebuilt so that movements of airport trains to and from the Relief Lines will not conflict with those on the Main Lines.

On the Great Eastern, the relocated and much enlarged Pudding Mill Lane DLR station was reopened on 28 April 2014. This facilitated the access of Crossrail trains to the Great Eastern main line, which they are to reach by passing beneath the DLR viaduct. Major reconstruction is being undertaken at Ilford and Romford and platform extensions are being built as necessary.

The Southeastern is being four tracked east of Plumstead, where Crossrail comes to the surface, with the new tracks on the north side. There will be 25kV ac electrification of the Crossrail tracks only (the others are DC third rail).

The terminal design at Abbey Wood, which is being completely rebuilt, allows for possible future continuation to Ebbsfleet, should that later be considered desirable.

Signalling

There is a new Railway Operations Centre (ROC) in Romford. The western end of Crossrail will be operated from the Thames Valley signalling centre at Didcot, which is also an ROC. In the central area (the TfL owned section), Computer Based Train Control (CBTC) with Automatic Train Operation (ATO) will be controlled from Romford, as will the southern branch to Abbey Wood.

The Upminster IECC is the first of the existing signalling installations to be transferred into Romford ROC, to be followed progressively by others and by Liverpool Street IECC in 2019. It may be of interest to note that under Network Rail's present plans Romford ROC will become the only such installation in Greater London; nationally there will be a total of 12 ROCs.

Trains

The 65 Crossrail Class 345 trains are being built by Bombardier at Derby. These are being 100% publicly funded, and are described as a further step on from the Bombardier Class 378s in use on London Overground. Each train will be made up of nine cars totalling 200m in length. They will be provided with air-conditioning and walk through connections between the cars and fitted with real time on-train information systems. The aim is the best technical train possible, offering the right value for money. This will be a lightweight design with an emphasis on energy efficiency. There is an option to purchase a further 18 trains.

The contract with Bombardier covers the supply, delivery and maintenance (for 32 years) of 65 new trains and a depot at Old Oak Common. Train maintenance will be carried out here and at Ilford, with additional facilities expected to be provided at Plumstead. This will minimise empty running for train positioning purposes. The first train is expected to appear in May 2017, with delivery followed by testing, staff training (train crew and maintenance staff) and introduction into service progressively.

Further development of the National Rail system is under consideration, and this section sets out the schemes involving National Railways that would appear most likely to be adopted, at least initially.

Crossrail western end

There is a modest embarrassment of getting better use out of the western end of Crossrail. If around half of the total service planned is not needed west of Paddington during the off-peak, are there alternative ideas?

The advent of HS2 is intended to create a station at Old Oak Common, which might provide substantial volumes of interchange. It depends also on additional station(s) being provided here on one or more of the following:

- Crossrail (Relief Lines)
- Great Western (Fast Lines)
- North London line
- West London line.

In each case, if built, how many will use them, and for what purposes? What new track alignments will be needed?

Some HS2 users are expected to see Old Oak Common and Crossrail offering worthwhile alternative routes to/from central London. How much traffic might be generated to/from Heathrow? Or to/from the West of England, South Wales, or Oxford and beyond? In the case of the latter, there is an advanced proposal for a western rail link from Heathrow to the Great Western main line towards Reading. There is also at least the possibility of another link in the opposite direction, to the South Western lines. In another sense altogether, economic regeneration of the area around Old Oak might in itself generate considerable traffic.

It would also be feasible to create a new connection for a western facing junction from Crossrail to the West Coast main line. A study into the issues involved is presently under way, with a provisional service destination of Tring.

Crossrail 2

Future projections, whether of population, employment or housing growth, come from several sources. Where is the place of the rail transport providers in enabling these to take place? The Mayor of London is one of those with major expansion in mind; here consideration is given to what might seem one of the more immediate priorities, that of Crossrail 2.

Crossrail 2 follows the approach of Crossrail 1 in linking up existing radial rail lines, in this case the Lea Valley lines originating from London Liverpool Street and some of the main line suburban services from London Waterloo, and building a new underground (but full sized) line between them.

Crossrail 2 is seen as the most important major investment project to be developed.

The favoured route for Crossrail 2 is from the Lea Valley north of Tottenham Hale and also from New Southgate alongside the GN line station. The two routes, both underground, merge before reaching Dalston Junction; thence with stations at Angel, Euston St Pancras (one station with two exits), Tottenham Court Road, Victoria, King's Road Chelsea, Clapham Junction, Tooting Broadway and Wimbledon, thence over the existing South Western lines to destinations such as Epsom or Twickenham.

The next stage is to refine the scheme and safeguard the route, with the aim of consulting on a single preferred route option in September 2015.

The incidence of both fast trains and stopping trains on the two track Lea Valley makes the introduction of more frequent stopping services difficult. It may be that some reinstallation of the second pair of tracks which once existed from Copper Mill Junction (south of Tottenham Hale) as far as Pickett's Lock (between Angel Road and Ponders End), or perhaps further north, will need to be undertaken in future. This would enable local services to be enhanced and the Stansted Express service to live up to its name. A nominal opening date of 2030 has been proposed by the Mayor of London.

RAIL SERVICES TO LONDON'S AIRPORTS

Airport station	*Service provider*	*Distance to central London*		*Time*
Heathrow T1,2,3	Heathrow Express	15 miles	Paddington	15 mins
Heathrow T1,2,3	Heathrow Connect	15 miles	Paddington	32 mins
Heathrow T1,2,3	London Underground	16 miles	Piccadilly Circus	48 mins
Heathrow T1,2,3	Crossrail 1	18 miles	Farringdon	32 mins
Gatwick Airport	Southern	27 miles	Victoria	30 mins
Gatwick Airport	Thameslink	28 miles	Farringdon	42 mins
Stansted Airport	Greater Anglia	37 miles	Liverpool Street	45 mins
Luton Airport Parkway*	Thameslink	31 miles	Farringdon	38 mins
Luton Airport Parkway*	East Midlands Trains	30 miles	St Pancras	19 mins
London City Airport	Docklands Light Rly	7 miles	Bank	21 mins
Southend Airport	Greater Anglia	40 miles	Liverpool Street	53 mins

* Then by dedicated bus connection to airport terminal

Journey times are those from central London, using the fastest off-peak trains at present. Service frequency is, of course, variable.

The new status of Farringdon is worthy of note. By 2019, it will have direct rail services to Heathrow by Crossrail, Gatwick by Thameslink and Luton by Thameslink plus bus. It is already possible to reach both Stansted and Southend airports from Farringdon with only one change of train at Liverpool Street, though London City Airport is a little trickier.

Stansted Express services have one stop en route, at Tottenham Hale, where there is interchange with the Victoria line. Stansted bound trains stop there to pick up only. Further south, 379.019 passes through Bethnal Green. *Kim Rennie*

The railways of London Underground may be divided into two distinct types. First are those known as the subsurface lines, which were originally steam operated. They are the Metropolitan, District, Circle and Hammersmith & City lines. These were built by cut-and-cover construction, which was largely complete by the end of the 19th century.

Developing technology allowed the building of the deep level railways in bored tunnels, hence the origin of the word 'tube'. These were always electrified and needed lifts (or later escalators) for passenger access. The tube lines, nowadays known as the deep tube lines, constitute the remainder of the network.

In recent years, the Underground has carried increasing numbers, which reached 1,305 million passengers in 2014/15 on a network of 402km. This was over 2.5 times the numbers carried of 0.498 billion in 1982, the lowest in the post war years. Since 2003, London Underground has been a wholly owned subsidiary of Transport for London.

London Underground serves 270 stations and the passenger fleet consists of 4,283 cars. Trains are made up of four, six, seven or eight cars, according to line; there are no longer any places where trains shorter than standard for that line are used. The busiest station in terms of annual entries plus exits is Oxford Circus with 99 million passengers in 2014. It is followed by King's Cross St Pancras with 92 million, Waterloo with 91 million and Victoria with 87 million.

As might be anticipated, the 10 least used stations with under 1 million passengers per annum are on the outer reaches of the Metropolitan, or the Essex end of the Central line plus, for some reason, North Ealing. Included are all the intermediate stations between Woodford and Hainault, with the wooden spoon, as it were, falling to Roding Valley. This station had just over a quarter of a million passengers during the year.

Of the route owned or managed by London Underground, 8% consists of subsurface cut-and-cover construction, 37% is in deep level tube, and 55% is above ground.

DM 96038 of 1996 Jubilee line stock is in the platform at Kilburn with a southbound service, being overtaken by a Metropolitan line train of S8 stock with DM 21054 at the rear. *Kim Rennie*

Bakerloo

The name was coined from the original Baker Street & Waterloo Railway, the first sections of which opened in 1906. Today, services are provided by 36 trains of the ageing 1972 MkII stock and subsequent conversions from other similar stock, all of which were built by Metro-Cammell. The depot is at Stonebridge Park. At the northern end of the line, trains from Elephant & Castle emerge from tunnel at Queen's Park, where many terminate. Others are projected over Network Rail tracks to Harrow & Wealdstone. Services on this section on the same tracks are those from London Euston to Watford Junction, provided by London Overground. The line from Harrow & Wealdstone to Elephant & Castle is 23km in length and serves 25 stations.

Bakerloo trains nowadays proceed no further north than Harrow & Wealdstone. On 17 May 2012, 1972 MkII car no 3234 leaves the reversal siding here to take up a working to Elephant & Castle. *Kim Rennie*

The interior of 1972 MkII Bakerloo line stock is certainly showing its age. One of the less attractive features of these trains is the lack of armrests, which were removed many years ago following vandalism. *Kim Rennie*

Central

The Central London Railway was, in 1900, the first tube line to open in the West End and ran between Shepherd's Bush and Bank via Oxford Circus. There are 85 trains, which are formed of 1992 stock built by BREL at Derby and are based at Hainault or Ruislip depots. Route extensions take the Central line to Ealing Broadway and West Ruislip in the west, and Epping or Woodford via Hainault in the east. An extension to Ongar was closed in 1994; part of this is now operated by the Epping-Ongar Railway preservation company. The tunnelled section of the Central line runs from White City to Stratford, followed by a short tunnel towards Leyton and a more lengthy tunnel from Leytonstone to Newbury Park. There is also a short tunnel between Grange Hill and Chigwell. The full line is 74km in length and serves 49 stations.

Circle

With the help of some prodding from Parliament, the Inner Circle was completed in 1884; it was in effect a joint Metropolitan Railway & District Railway venture. With the exception of short lengths of line between High Street Kensington and Gloucester Road, and between Aldgate and Tower Hill, the Circle shares all its route with other subsurface lines. Since 2009, when the present service pattern was introduced, it has an open air section between Paddington and Hammersmith. Operation is with 53 trains of air-conditioned S7 stock. These seven car trains were built by Bombardier at Derby for a fleet shared with the Hammersmith & City and the District's Edgware Road–Wimbledon line. The depot is at Hammersmith. The line is 27km in length and serves 36 stations.

Opposite: Interior and exterior views of the Central line's 1992 Tube stock, its large windows provided for the long open sections of the line out to Essex. The train exterior view is at Woodford. *Capital Transport, Kim Rennie*

An outer-rail Circle line S7 stock train for Edgware Road arrives at Monument with DM 21305 in the lead. Monument and Bank are connected by subsurface walkways and escalators and between them boast 10 platforms. *Chris Wilson*

District

Originating with a section between South Kensington and Westminster in 1868, the District main line is characterised by the imbalance between a single line to Upminster in the east, and branches to Ealing Broadway, Richmond, Wimbledon and Kensington Olympia in the west. The large fleet of Metro-Cammell D stock of 1980 is in the process of being replaced by 80 trains of S7 stock built by Bombardier. Main depots are at Ealing Common and Upminster. The line is 64km in length and serves 60 stations. There are two bridges over the Thames, on the Wimbledon and Richmond branches. Most of the displaced D stock has been sold to Vivarail, a company intending to refurbish them and convert them to diesel power for use on secondary lines of the national railway system.

Hammersmith & City

The line between Paddington and Hammersmith opened in 1864, a joint venture between the Metropolitan and the Great Western company. Beyond Whitechapel (where it is no longer possible to terminate), the line continues in tunnel, but east of Bow Road it is entirely in the open air. The only section over which the Hammersmith & City is now the sole service provider is that between Liverpool Street and Aldgate East. Services are provided by S7 stock. The line is 29km in length and serves 29 stations from Hammersmith to the eastern terminus at Barking. It has a depot at Hammersmith.

From mid-2016 all sub-surface mainline gauge trains on the Underground will be of S stock. A Hammersmith & City line seven-car train is seen at Ladbroke Grove. *Kim Rennie*

Metropolitan

This, the original section of the Underground, opened in 1863 between Paddington and Farringdon. Today, there are four routes from Aldgate and Baker Street, to Uxbridge, Amersham, Chesham and Watford. From Finchley Road north, the line is in the open. The line is 67km in length and serves 34 stations. All 58 trains in the fleet are formed of S8 stock and the depot is at Neasden.

The S stock is not over-provided with seats and as a concession to the longer distance passengers from Amersham, Watford and Uxbridge the S8 trains incorporate some transverse seating. *Kim Rennie*

Jubilee

The creation of what is now the Jubilee line started with the opening of the Stanmore branch of the Metropolitan north of Wembley Park in 1932. That and what became the centre tracks of the section to Baker Street was part of the Bakerloo line, transferring to the Jubilee when that was constructed to Green Park in 1979 and to Stratford in 1999. A fleet of what is now made up of 63 1996 stock seven car trains has been built by Alstom. Depots are at Stratford Market and Neasden, the latter shared with the Metropolitan. Services operate between Stanmore and Stratford. The line is 36km in length and serves 27 stations.

The 1996 stock on the Jubilee line and the 1995 stock are almost identical. The Northern line's southern terminus of Morden is seen from above the tunnel mouth, demonstrating just how little of this end of the journey is made in the daylight. A train of 1995 stock with DM 51614 at the rear is arriving in Platform 5. *Kim Rennie*

Northern

This line has a complex history, having been derived from the City & South London Railway dating from 1890 and the Charing Cross, Euston & Hampstead Railway from 1907. Major reconstructions over the years led to the enlargement of the City & South London, judicious new sections joining the two systems, and absorption of parts of the then London & North Eastern Railway in 1940/1. The present Northern line is 58km in length and serves 50 stations. There are three northern branches to Edgware, Mill Hill East and High Barnet. Uniquely for tube railways, there are two separate routes in the central area, via Charing Cross and via Bank. The southern terminus is at Morden. The line is underground apart from the Morden terminus and the sections East Finchley and north, and Golders Green and north. There is a tunnel between Hendon Central and Colindale. Line depots are at Golders Green and Morden. Operation is by 106 six-car trains of 1995 tube stock, built by Alstom.

Piccadilly

Originally two separate companies, the Great Northern, Piccadilly & Brompton opened in 1906 between Finsbury Park and Hammersmith. Subsequent extensions took it to Cockfosters in the north and to Uxbridge and Heathrow in the west. The line is 74km in length and serves 53 stations. The section between Arnos Grove and Barons Court is continuously underground, as is that from Hounslow West onwards, apart from a very short section above ground to cross the River Crane. Southgate station is also in tunnel. From Cockfosters in the north, the line divides at Acton Town for Rayners Lane and Uxbridge or for Hounslow and Heathrow Airport. Trains to the latter can call either at Terminal 4 and Terminals 1,2,3 (via the terminal loop and in that order), or Terminals 1,2,3 and Terminal 5. Metro-Cammell of Birmingham supplied the fleet of 86 six-car trains which now form the Piccadilly fleet. These are 1973 stock, constructed with airport passengers and their luggage in mind. Planned replacement of these heavily used trains with new trains has been delayed about 10 years by financial constraints. Depots are at Cockfosters and Northfields.

The Piccadilly line is first in line to receive the next generation of tube stock – currently being referred to as the New Tube for London (NTfL), despite its trains not being the oldest. The 1973 stock, an example of which is seen at Stamford Brook on the fast section of the line between Hammersmith and Acton Town, does however serve some of the busiest parts of the system. *Kim Rennie*

Victoria

A long time in the planning, the Victoria line opened in sections between 1968 and 1971; it used Automatic Train Operation from the outset. Every station, save only Pimlico, has interchange facilities with another National Rail or Underground line. The line is 21km in length and serves 16 stations from Walthamstow Central to Brixton. It is wholly underground, apart from the depot at Northumberland Park. The line is operated by 47 trains of 2009 tube stock, each of 8 cars. These were built by Bombardier in Derby.

A train of 2009 stock arrives at Brixton, the southern terminus of the Victoria line. Northumberland Park depot is the only above ground location on this line. *Jason Cross*

It is 8 August 2013 at Bank's no 8 platform and 1992 stock DM 65505 forms the nearest vehicle of a Waterloo & City service. The platform hump to assist access is readily visible; there are not so many customers around at 13:17:52 on a Thursday. *Chris Wilson*

Waterloo & City

The line between Waterloo and Bank was opened in 1898 by an offshoot of the London & South Western Railway. Its main purpose in life was to take those arriving on main line trains at Waterloo to and from the City.

Trains comprise five 4-car variants of the Central line 1992 stock and are based at a depot at Waterloo.

The line, which is completely underground, is 2.4km in length and serves two stations only. It became part of London Underground in 1994.

The Waterloo & City departure platform at Waterloo on 8 August 2013 sees DM no 65505 arriving to pick up its passengers before leaving for Bank. Separate arrival and departure platforms at termini are unusual, although a similar arrangement has been adopted for the Piccadilly line's Heathrow Terminal 5 station. *Chris Wilson*

Station reconstruction

Extensive station reconstruction is being undertaken at a number of London Underground stations. Most of this is to cater for fast increasing passenger numbers, but also to accommodate either Crossrail 1 or Thameslink within the overall premises. Further works will be needed should a decision be made to proceed with HS2 and/or Crossrail 2. Major works are presently under way at, for instance, Farringdon, Tottenham Court Road and Victoria, with more planned. An example is Bank. The various platforms at Bank station are spread over a considerable distance and the station is to undergo major reconstruction. The centrepiece will be the southbound Northern line platform turned into a concourse between the two Northern line tracks. A new tunnel and platform is to be built for southbound trains. A travelator will be constructed in the concourse area to speed passengers on their way from the District line at Monument in the south to the Central line at Bank in the north. A new station entrance is to be built in Walbrook, for step free access to the Waterloo & City line. Major works that remain outstanding are the long-delayed resignalling of the subsurface lines.

Line extensions

The Metropolitan branch beyond Croxley is being diverted to serve new stations at Cassiobridge and Watford Vicarage Road. It will then join the existing London Overground route from London Euston, with Metropolitan trains calling at Watford High Street and terminating at Watford Junction. The present Watford (Met) station will be closed.

A Northern line extension is to be constructed from the existing Kennington loop on the Charing Cross branch to a new station at Nine Elms; the line will terminate at Battersea.

Possible routes and traffic objectives for a southern extension of the Bakerloo have been under discussion and the favourite option identified as one via Camberwell and Lewisham to Hayes (Kent) and Beckenham or Bromley.

Further expansion of Heathrow Airport, should that happen, will have implications for Piccadilly line service provision.

New Tube for London

Both the Bakerloo and Piccadilly stock are becoming in need of replacement, while the Central and Waterloo & City line stock is 23 years old. An expanded network will need more trains, too.

Trains for the New Tube for London project will deliver:

- Higher capacity
- Increased reliability and energy efficiency
- Saloon cooling on deep tube lines for the first time
- All double doorways and walk through interiors
- Capability for a higher level of automation.

These trains will be articulated and with shorter bodies. This will reduce the number of wheelsets needed, allow closer coupling of vehicles and reduce platform to train stepping distances on curved platforms.

In 2016 it is intended to award a contract for the Piccadilly line fleet, with options for Bakerloo, Central and Waterloo & City lines. The first new trains for the Piccadilly are expected to enter service in 2023.

Weekend working

On a more modest scale, it is intended to introduce all night working, Friday and Saturday nights only, on the Jubilee and Victoria lines, plus parts of the Piccadilly, Central and Northern lines in September 2015. Night time operation will be extended to the East London line of London Overground in 2017, with the subsurface lines and Docklands Light Railway following by 2021.

The New Tube for London is expected to begin service in 2023 on the Piccadilly Line.

The Docklands Light Railway can be traced back to 1982 with the setting up of the London Docklands Development Commission, whose aim was the rejuvenation and development of what had become a run down industrial area. A main requirement was adequate transport.

The original section of the DLR was from Tower Gateway on the very edge of the City of London to what became Canary Wharf and then Island Gardens, with a northern branch to Stratford. This was a minimum budget railway. It opened in 1987, with a total of 11 two section vehicles to provide the entire service for 15 stations spread over 13km of line.

The DLR has since been extended to, successively, a new city terminus of Bank 1991, from Poplar to Beckton 1994, from Mudchute to Greenwich and Lewisham 1999, from Canning Town to London City Airport 2005 and Woolwich Arsenal 2009, and from Canning Town to Stratford International in 2011. Only the 2km length of line between Bow Church and Stratford has any single track sections. Poplar is at the centre of this fully segregated system and the original small depot, later supplemented by the much larger Beckton Depot, reached by a spur from Gallions Reach. The system control centre is also situated here.

Of the 46 DLR stations, the largest is Canary Wharf with six platform faces and three tracks. The system carried 101 million passengers in 2013/14; the busiest station is Bank, followed by Canary Wharf and Canning Town.

There are now 149 broadly similar cars of types B90, B92, B2K and B07, built between 1991 and 2010 in Belgium or Germany. Maximum speed is 80 km/h. All are 2-section articulated sets, and most services are now provided by three sets, joined. That makes the trains 90 metres long, which has been associated with extensive upgrading, not least of platform lengths.

The present operators are Keolis Amey Docklands Ltd, whose franchise runs until 2021.

Train services run from 05:30 – 00:30, or 07:00-23:30 on Sundays. Routes are as follows:

- Tower Gateway – Poplar – Canning Town – Beckton
- Bank – Poplar – Canning Town – Woolwich Arsenal
- Bank – Canary Wharf – Lewisham
- Stratford – Poplar – Canary Wharf – Lewisham
- Stratford International – Canning Town – Beckton
- Stratford International – Canning Town – Woolwich Arsenal

This is a third rail 750v dc system with underside contact and moving block signalling. This has the capacity to provide a service to Bank/Tower Gateway stations together, including the flat junctions, of 29 trains per hour. Trains are normally driven automatically, except in depot areas.

There is a Passenger Service Agent on board every train, but payment must be made before boarding. Stations, other than those deemed to be underground (Bank, Cutty Sark, Island Gardens and Woolwich Arsenal), are generally unstaffed. There are Information Points at Canary Wharf and London City Airport.

The Emirates Air Line cable cars are operated by the Docklands Light Railway. These run from Emirates Royal Docks (close to DLR Royal Victoria station), crossing the Thames to Emirates Greenwich Peninsula (close to North Greenwich Jubilee line station).

Opposite top: On 28 May 2015 Docklands Light Railway Class B07 car no 147 is approaching Shadwell alongside the LT&S main line. *Capital Transport*

Opposite: Docklands Light Railway Class B92 unit 80 leads a train into Pudding Mill Lane station via track diverted in connection with Crossrail construction. *Capital Transport*

DLR
147

APARTMENTS
FOR SALE IN
STRATFORD
DLR
80

London Tramlink was designed to bring the advantages of a partially segregated and modern rail-based urban transport system to a busy London suburban setting.

The centre of this 28km system with 39 stops is a compact clockwise only route around central Croydon. This runs on street and in the course of negotiating this Tramlink calls at or has a stop adjacent to East Croydon station, West Croydon station and West Croydon bus station. All tram services must use all or part of this route when serving the outlying areas.

Today, services run as follows:

Route 1 Elmers End and Croydon
Route 2 Beckenham Junction and Croydon
Route 3 Wimbledon, Croydon, New Addington
Route 4 Elmers End, Croydon and Therapia Lane (not evenings or Sundays)

Much of Tramlink is double track, running on former railway alignments wherever these are available. What was once the Wimbledon to West Croydon branch railway was single track with limited passing opportunities. Much of this has been made into double track as an essential prelude to increasing service frequencies.

Leaving central Croydon, Tramlink is not segregated from the road until it reaches Sandilands, where a steep descent to the former rail track in cutting enables trams to turn north towards Elmers End and Beckenham Junction. Beyond Arena, the branch to Elmers End is single track. The line to Beckenham Junction becomes single where it runs in parallel with the (singled) National Rail branch from Crystal Palace. There are two intermediate passing places on this section.

The line running south to New Addington diverges from the route of the former Elmers End to Sanderstead railway after negotiating three short tunnels and runs on new construction to the terminus at the centre of this residential area.

There are substantial numbers of footpath or road level crossings throughout. At Addiscombe station, formerly the site of Bingham Road railway station which was on an embankment, Tramlink is now at ground level.

At Wimbledon, Tramlink uses Platform 10 of the main station, operated by South West Trains. Other users are Thameslink and London Underground. A second terminating place is being provided by extending the line past the existing platform track and then bringing it in next to the platform.

This is a 750v dc overhead system. The Tramlink fleet consists of 24 3-section 30.1 metre trams built by Bombardier in Austria for the opening of the system in 2000, supplemented by two batches of 5-section Variobahn trams from Stadler in Germany. These are longer, at 32.4 metres. The first six were delivered in 2011/12. All have disc, regenerative and magnetic track brakes. The earlier trams have 70 seats, the Stadlers 74. Platform height is 350mm above rail level.

Therapia Lane depot, which has extensive maintenance facilities, stabling for all the fleet and the system control room, is on the Wimbledon line.

The Tramlink network is operated by Tram Operations Ltd, a subsidiary of First Group, under a 30-year operating agreement with London Tramlink.

Opposite top: George Street, Croydon. On the right is a Route 4 tram to Therapia Lane using a 5-section Stadler vehicle 2557. On the left is Route 2 tram to Beckenham Junction, using one of the original Bombardier 3-section trams, 2552. The slight hump in the background marks where the road and tramway rise slightly to cross the Brighton main line. *John Bradshaw*

Opposite: Beddington Lane sees Tram no 2542 in a somewhat startling red Turkish Airlines advertising livery on a Route 3 service to Wimbledon. The low platforms used on this system are apparent in this view. *John Bradshaw*

Beckenham Junction 2
4 Therapia Lane
2553
2557
OFFICES TO

Wimbledon 3
2542
TURKISHAIRLINES.COM
Beddington Lane

LEVEL CROSSINGS IN GREATER LONDON

This list covers road level crossings in the Greater London Area. Footpath only crossings are not included, and those giving access to private estates and/or on freight only lines are generally omitted. Nearly all are monitored by CCTV, either locally or remotely. A few still retain manual control. In each case the name of the nearest passenger station is included for identification purposes; if there is no road name, the crossing is close to that station. The names given here may thus differ from the 'official' name.

This list reflects the situation in mid-2015, but readers are reminded that a reduction in the numbers of level crossings is a continuing aim.

London, Tilbury & Southend
Rainham, Ferry Lane
Rainham, Manor Way

Great Eastern
Brimsdown
Bush Hill Park, Lincoln Road
Enfield Lock
Highams Park
Northumberland Park

North London Line
Acton Central
South Acton, Bollo Lane, Richmond Line
South Acton, Bollo Lane, Kew Line

West London Line
Willesden Junction, Mitre Bridge

South Western
Barnes, Vine Road, Hounslow Line,
Barnes, Vine Road, Richmond Line
Chiswick, Grove Park
Feltham West
Hampton, Percy Road
Isleworth, Wood Lane
Mortlake, Sheen Lane
Mortlake, White Hart
Motspur Park
New Malden, Elm Road
North Sheen
Raynes Park, West Barnes Lane
Strawberry Hill

South Central
Mitcham Eastfields

South Eastern
Charlton, Charlton Lane

On 24 April 2015 no 455.721 is seen arriving at Mortlake with a South West Trains Kingston Roundabout service which originated at London Waterloo. At this stage it shows a destination of Strawberry Hill. The train is passing over the level crossing at the platform ends, one of a considerable number in this general area. *Capital Transport*

5721

STATIONS IN GREATER LONDON AND STATION OPERATOR 2015

The company that operates the station may have the trains of other companies calling.
The only stations included outside Greater London are those served by London Underground or London Overground and are marked *
National Rail London termini carry the name London Euston, etc. London Underground use plain Euston.

Abbey Wood	Southeastern
Acton Central	London Overground
Acton Main Line	First Great Western
Acton Town	London Underground
Albany Park	Southeastern
Aldgate	London Underground
Aldgate East	London Underground
Alexandra Palace	Great Northern
Alperton	London Underground
Amersham*	London Underground
Anerley	London Overground
Angel	London Underground
Angel Road	Greater Anglia
Archway	London Underground
Arnos Grove	London Underground
Arsenal	London Underground
Baker Street	London Underground
Balham	London Underground
Balham	Southern
Bank	London Underground
Barbican	London Underground
Barking	c2c
Barkingside	London Underground
Barnehurst	Southeastern
Barnes	South West Trains
Barnes Bridge	South West Trains
Barons Court	London Underground
Battersea Park	Southern
Bayswater	London Underground
Beckenham Hill	Thameslink
Beckenham Junction	Southeastern
Becontree	London Underground
Bellingham	Southeastern
Belmont	Southern
Belsize Park	London Underground
Belvedere	Southeastern
Bermondsey	London Underground
Berrylands	South West Trains
Bethnal Green LU	London Underground
Bethnal Green NR	London Overground
Bexley	Southeastern
Bexleyheath	Southeastern
Bickley	Southeastern
Birkbeck	Southern
Blackfriars LU	London Underground
Blackheath	Southeastern
Blackhorse Road	London Underground
Bond Street	London Underground
Borough	London Underground
Boston Manor	London Underground
Bounds Green	London Underground
Bow Road	London Underground
Bowes Park	Great Northern
Brent Cross	London Underground

The large new station building at Farringdon is directly opposite the C.W. Clark Metropolitan line building in Cowcross Street. Passenger numbers using Farringdon will surge with the opening of Crossrail and the enhanced Thameslink services for which this new station has been built. *Capital Transport*

Station	Operator
Brentford	South West Trains
Brentwood*	TfL Rail (XR)
Brimsdown	Greater Anglia
Brixton LU	London Underground
Brixton NR	Southeastern
Brockley	London Overground
Bromley North	Southeastern
Bromley South	Southeastern
Bromley-by-Bow	London Underground
Brondesbury	London Overground
Brondesbury Park	London Overground
Bruce Grove	London Overground
Buckhurst Hill*	London Underground
Burnt Oak	London Underground
Bush Hill Park	London Overground
Bushey*	London Overground
Caledonian Road	London Underground
Caledonian Road & Barnsbury	London Overground
Cambridge Heath	London Overground
Camden Road	London Overground
Camden Town	London Underground
Canada Water	London Underground
Canary Wharf	London Underground
Canning Town	London Underground
Cannon Street LU	London Underground
Canonbury	London Overground
Canons Park	London Underground
Carpenders Park*	London Overground
Carshalton	Southern
Castle Bar Park	First Great Western
Catford	Southeastern
Catford Bridge	Southeastern
Chadwell Heath	TfL Rail (XR)
Chalfont & Latimer*	London Underground
Chalk Farm	London Underground
Chancery Lane	London Underground
Charing Cross	London Underground
Charlton	Southeastern
Cheam	Southern
Chelsfield	Southeastern
Chesham*	London Underground
Cheshunt*	Greater Anglia
Chessington North	South West Trains
Chessington South	South West Trains
Chigwell*	London Underground
Chingford	London Overground
Chislehurst	Southeastern
Chiswick	South West Trains
Chiswick Park	London Underground
Chorleywood*	London Underground
City Thameslink	Thameslink
Clapham Common	London Underground
Clapham High Street	London Overground
Clapham Junction	South West Trains
Clapham North	London Underground
Clapham South	London Underground
Clapton	London Overground
Clock House	Southeastern
Cockfosters	London Underground
Colindale	London Underground
Colliers Wood	London Underground
Coulsdon Town	Southern
Covent Garden	London Underground
Crayford	Southeastern
Cricklewood	Thameslink
Crofton Park	Southeastern
Crouch Hill	London Overground
Croxley*	London Underground
Crystal Palace	London Overground
Dagenham Dock	c2c
Dagenham East	London Underground
Dagenham Heathway	London Underground
Dalston Junction	London Overground
Dalston Kingsland	London Overground
Debden*	London Underground
Denmark Hill	Thameslink
Deptford	Southeastern
Dollis Hill	London Underground
Drayton Green	First Great Western
Drayton Park	Great Northern
Ealing Broadway	First Great Western
Earl's Court	London Underground
Earlsfield	South West Trains
East Acton	London Underground
East Croydon	Southern
East Dulwich	Southern
East Finchley	London Underground
East Ham	London Underground
East Putney	London Underground
Eastcote	London Underground
Eden Park	Southeastern
Edgware	London Underground
Edgware Road Bakerloo	London Underground
Edgware Road subsurface	London Underground
Elephant & Castle LU	London Underground
Elephant & Castle NR	Thameslink
Elm Park	London Underground
Elmers End	Southeastern
Elmstead Woods	Southeastern
Eltham	Southeastern
Embankment	London Underground
Emerson Park	London Overground
Enfield Chase	Great Northern
Enfield Lock	Greater Anglia
Enfield Town	London Overground
Epping*	London Underground
Erith	Southeastern
Essex Road	Great Northern
Euston LU	London Underground
Euston Square	London Underground
Fairlop	London Underground
Falconwood	Southeastern
Farringdon	London Underground
Feltham	South West Trains
Finchley Central	London Underground
Finchley Road	London Underground
Finchley Road & Frognal	London Overground
Finsbury Park LU	London Underground
Finsbury Park NR	Great Northern
Forest Gate	TfL Rail (XR)
Forest Hill	London Overground
Fulham Broadway	London Underground
Fulwell	South West Trains
Gants Hill*	London Underground
Gipsy Hill	Southern
Gloucester Road	London Underground
Golders Green	London Underground
Goldhawk Road	London Underground
Goodge Street	London Underground
Goodmayes	TfL Rail (XR)
Gordon Hill	Great Northern
Gospel Oak	London Overground
Grange Hill*	London Underground
Grange Park	Great Northern
Great Portland Street	London Underground
Green Park	London Underground
Greenford	London Underground
Greenwich	Southeastern
Grove Park	Southeastern
Gunnersbury	London Underground
Hackbridge	Southern
Hackney Central	London Overground
Hackney Downs	London Overground
Hackney Wick	London Overground

Station	Operator
Hadley Wood	Great Northern
Haggerston	London Overground
Hainault	London Underground
Hammersmith D&P	London Underground
Hammersmith H&C	London Underground
Hampstead	London Underground
Hampstead Heath	London Overground
Hampton	South West Trains
Hampton Wick	South West Trains
Hanger Lane	London Underground
Hanwell	First Great Western
Harlesden	London Underground
Harold Wood	TfL Rail (XR)
Harringay	Great Northern
Harringay Green Lanes	London Overground
Harrow & Wealdstone	London Underground
Harrow-on-the-Hill	London Underground
Hatch End	London Overground
Hatton Cross	London Underground
Hayes	Southeastern
Hayes & Harlington	First Great Western
Headstone Lane	London Overground
Heathrow T1, 2, 3 HX	Heathrow Express
Heathrow T4 HX	Heathrow Express
Heathrow T5	Heathrow Express
Heathrow Terminal 4	London Underground
Heathrow Terminals 1,2,3	London Underground
Hendon	Thameslink
Hendon Central	London Underground
Herne Hill	Southeastern
High Barnet	London Underground
High Street Kensington	London Underground
Highams Park	London Overground
Highbury & Islington	London Underground
Highgate	London Underground
Hillingdon	London Underground
Hither Green	Southeastern
Holborn	London Underground
Holland Park	London Underground
Holloway Road	London Underground
Homerton	London Overground
Honor Oak Park	London Overground
Honslow	South West Trains
Hornchurch	London Underground
Hornsey	Great Northern
Hounslow Central	London Underground
Hounslow East	London Underground
Hounslow West	London Underground
Hoxton	London Overground
Hyde Park Corner	London Underground
Ickenham	London Underground
Ilford	TfL Rail (XR)
Imperial Wharf	London Overground
Isleworth	South West Trains
Kenley	Southern
Kennington	London Underground
Kensal Green	London Underground
Kensal Rise	London Overground
Kensington Olympia	London Overground
Kentish Town	London Underground
Kentish Town West	London Overground
Kenton	London Underground
Kew Bridge	South West Trains
Kew Gardens	London Underground
Kidbrooke	Southeastern
Kilburn	London Underground
Kilburn High Road	London Overground
Kilburn Park	London Underground
King's Cross St Pancras	London Underground
Kingsbury	London Underground
Kingston	South West Trains
Knightsbridge	London Underground
Knockholt	Southeastern
Ladbroke Grove	London Underground
Ladywell	Southeastern
Lambeth North	London Underground
Lancaster Gate	London Underground
Latimer Road	London Underground
Lee	Southeastern
Leicester Square	London Underground
Lewisham	Southeastern
Leystonstone High Road	London Overground
Leyton	London Underground
Leyton Midland Road	London Overground
Leytonstone	London Underground
Limehouse	c2c
Liverpool Street LU	London Underground
London Blackfriars	Thameslink
London Bridge LU	London Underground
London Bridge NR	Network Rail
London Cannon Street	Network Rail
London Charing Cross	Network Rail
London Euston	Network Rail
London Fenchurch Street	Network Rail
London Fields	London Overground
London King's Cross	Network Rail
London Liverpool Street	Network Rail
London Marylebone	Chiltern Railways
London Paddington	Network Rail
London St Pancras International	Network Rail
London Victoria	Network Rail
London Waterloo	Network Rail
Loughborough Junction	Thameslink
Loughton*	London Underground
Lower Edmonton	London Overground
Lower Sydenham	Southeastern
Lower Sydenham	Southeastern
Maida Vale	London Underground
Malden Manor	South West Trains
Manor House	London Underground
Manor Park	TfL Rail (XR)
Mansion House	London Underground
Marble Arch	London Underground
Maryland	TfL Rail (XR)
Marylebone LU	London Underground
Maze Hill	Southeastern
Mile End	London Underground
Mill Hill Broadway	Thameslink
Mill Hill East	London Underground
Mitcham Junction	Southern
Monument	London Underground
Moor Park*	London Underground
Moorgate	London Underground
Morden	London Underground
Morden South	Thameslink
Mornington Crescent	London Underground
Mortlake	South West Trains
Motspur Park	South West Trains
Mottingham	Southeastern
Neasden	London Underground
New Barnet	Great Northern
New Beckenham	Southeastern
New Cross	Southeastern
New Cross Gate	London Overground
New Eltham	Southeastern
New Malden	South West Trains
New Southgate	Great Northern
Newbury Park	London Underground
Norbiton	South West Trains
Norbury	Southern
North Acton	London Underground
North Dulwich	Southern
North Ealing	London Underground
North Greenwich	London Underground

Station	Operator
North Harrow	London Underground
North Sheen	South West Trains
North Wembley	London Underground
Northfields	London Underground
Northolt	London Underground
Northolt Park	Chiltern Railways
Northumberland Park	Greater Anglia
Northwick Park	London Underground
Northwood	London Underground
Northwood Hills	London Underground
Norwood Junction	London Overground
Notting Hill Gate	London Underground
Nunhead	Thameslink
Oakleigh Park	Great Northern
Oakwood	London Underground
Old Street	London Underground
Orpington	Southeastern
Osterley	London Underground
Oval	London Underground
Oxford Circus	London Underground
Paddington	London Underground
Palmers Green	Great Northern
Park Royal	London Underground
Parsons Green	London Underground
Peckham Rye	Southern
Penge East	Southeastern
Penge West	London Overground
Perivale	London Underground
Petts Wood	Southeastern
Piccadilly Circus	London Underground
Pimlico	London Underground
Pinner	London Underground
Plaistow	London Underground
Plumstead	Southeastern
Ponders End	Greater Anglia
Preston Road	London Underground
Purley	Southern
Purley Oaks	Southern
Putney	South West Trains
Putney Bridge	London Underground
Queen's Park	London Underground
Queens Road, Battersea	South West Trains
Queen's Road, Peckham	Southern
Queensbury	London Underground
Queenstown Road, Battersea	South West Trains
Queensway	London Underground
Rainham	c2c
Ravensbourne	Thameslink
Ravenscourt Park	London Underground
Rayners Lane	London Underground
Raynes Park	South West Trains
Rectory Road	London Overground
Redbridge	London Underground
Reedham	Southern
Regent's Park	London Underground
Richmond	South West Trains
Rickmansworth*	London Underground
Riddlesdown	Southern
Roding Valley*	London Underground
Rotherhithe	London Overground
Royal Oak	London Underground
Ruislip	London Underground
Ruislip Manor	London Underground
Ruislip Gardens	London Underground
Russell Square	London Underground
Sanderstead	Southern
Seven Kings	TfL Rail (XR)
Seven Sisters	London Underground
Shadwell	London Overground
Shenfield*	Greater Anglia
Shepherd's Bush LU	London Underground
Shepherds Bush Market	London Underground
Shepherds Bush WLL	London Overground
Shoreditch High Street	London Overground
Shortlands	Southeastern
Sidcup	Southeastern
Silver Street	London Overground
Slade Green	Southeastern
Sloane Square	London Underground
Snaresbrook	London Underground
South Acton	London Overground
South Bermondsay	Southern
South Croydon	Southern
South Ealing	London Underground
South Greenford	First Great Western
South Hampstead	London Overground
South Harrow	London Underground
South Kensington	London Underground
South Kenton	London Underground
South Merton	Thameslink
South Ruislip LU	London Underground
South Ruislip NR	Chiltern Railways
South Tottenham	London Overground
South Wimbledon	London Underground
South Woodford	London Underground
Southall	First Great Western
Southbury	London Overground
Southfields	London Underground
Southgate	London Underground
Southwark	London Underground
St Helier	Thameslink
St James Street	London Overground
St James's Park	London Underground
St John's	Southeastern
St John's Wood	London Underground
St Margarets	South West Trains
St Mary Cray	Southeastern
St Pauls	London Underground
Stamford Brook	London Underground
Stamford Hill	London Overground
Stanmore	London Underground
Stepney Green	London Underground
Stockwell	London Underground
Stoke Newington	London Overground
Stonebridge Park	London Underground
Stratford	TfL Rail (XR)
Stratford International	Southeastern
Strawberry Hill	South West Trains
Streatham	Southern
Streatham Common	Southern
Sudbury & Harrow Road	Chiltern Railways
Sudbury Hill	London Underground
Sudbury Hill Harrow	Chiltern Railways
Sudbury Town	London Underground
Sundridge Park	Southeastern
Surbiton	South West Trains
Surrey Quays	London Overground
Sutton	Southern
Sutton Common	Thameslink
Swiss Cottage	London Underground
Sydenham	London Overground
Sydenham Hill	Southeastern
Syon Lane	South West Trains
Teddington	South West Trains
Temple	London Underground
Theobalds Grove*	London Overground
Theydon Bois*	London Underground
Thornton Heath	Southern
Tolworth	South West Trains
Tooting Bec	London Underground
Tooting Broadway	London Underground
Tottenham Court Road	London Underground
Tottenham Hale	London Underground
Totteridge & Whetstone	London Underground
Tower Hill	London Underground

Station	Operator
Tufnell Park	London Underground
Tulse Hill	Southern
Turkey Street	London Overground
Turnham Green	London Underground
Turnpike Lane	London Underground
Twickenham	South West Trains
Upminster	c2c
Upminster Bridge	London Underground
Upney	London Underground
Upper Holloway	London Overground
Upton Park	London Underground
Uxbridge	London Underground
Vauxhall LU	London Underground
Vauxhall NR	South West Trains
Victoria LU	London Underground
Walthamstow Central LU	London Underground
Walthamstow Central NR	London Overground
Wandsworth Common	Southern
Wandsworth Road	London Overground
Wandsworth Town	South West Trains
Wanstead	London Underground
Wanstead Park	London Overground
Wapping	London Overground
Warren Street	London Underground
Warwick Avenue	London Underground
Waterloo LU	London Underground
Watford (Met)*	London Underground
Watford High St*	London Overground
Watford Junction*	London Midland
Welling	Southeastern
Wembley Central	London Underground
Wembley Park	London Underground
Wembley Stadium	Chiltern Railways
West Acton	London Underground
West Brompton	London Underground
West Croydon	London Overground
West Drayton	First Great Western
West Dulwich	Southeastern
West Ealing	First Great Western
West Finchley	London Underground
West Ham	London Underground
West Hampstead LU	London Underground
West Hampstead NR	London Overground
West Hampstead Thameslink	Thameslink
West Harrow	London Underground
West Kensington	London Underground
West Norwood	Southern
West Ruislip LU	London Underground
West Ruislip NR	Chiltern Railways
West Sutton	Thameslink
West Wickham	Southeastern
Westbourne Park	London Underground
Westcombe Park	Southeastern
Westminster	London Underground
White City	London Underground
White Hart Lane	London Overground
Whitechapel	London Underground
Whitton	South West Trains
Willesden Green	London Underground
Willesden Junction	London Overground
Wimbledon	South West Trains
Wimbledon Chase	Thameslink
Wimbledon Park	London Underground
Winchmore Hill	Great Northern
Wood Green	London Underground
Wood Lane	London Underground
Wood Street	London Overground
Woodford	London Underground
Woodgrange Park	London Overground
Woodmansterne	Southern
Woodside Park	London Underground
Woolwich Arsenal	Southeastern
Woolwich Dockyard	Southeastern
Worcester Park	South West Trains

Total: 562 stations excluding DLR and Tramlink.

Waterloo station has had its concourse modernised in the recent past with a new parade of shops on the first floor accessed by escalators. *Kim Rennie*

Front cover photo: *Kim Rennie*
Title page photo: *Capital Transport*